The life and death of Thomas Wolsey, cardinal : once archbishop of York and Lord Chancellor of England

George Cavendish, Grace H. M Simpson

Nabu Public Domain Reprints:

You are holding a reproduction of an original work published before 1923 that is in the public domain in the United States of America, and possibly other countries. You may freely copy and distribute this work as no entity (individual or corporate) has a copyright on the body of the work. This book may contain prior copyright references, and library stamps (as most of these works were scanned from library copies). These have been scanned and retained as part of the historical artifact.

This book may have occasional imperfections such as missing or blurred pages, poor pictures, errant marks, etc. that were either part of the original artifact, or were introduced by the scanning process. We believe this work is culturally important, and despite the imperfections, have elected to bring it back into print as part of our continuing commitment to the preservation of printed works worldwide. We appreciate your understanding of the imperfections in the preservation process, and hope you enjoy this valuable book.

LIFE OF CARDINAL WOLSEY

THE LIFE AND DEATH
OF
THOMAS WOLSEY
CARDINAL
Once Archbishop of York and Lord Chancellor of England

CONTAINING

1. THE ORIGIN OF HIS PROMOTION, AND THE WAY HE TOOK TO OBTAIN IT
2. THE CONTINUANCE IN HIS MAGNIFICENCE
3. HIS NEGOTIATIONS CONCERNING THE PEACE WITH FRANCE AND THE NETHERLANDS
4. HIS FALL, DEATH, AND BURIAL

   WHEREIN ARE THINGS REMARKABLE FOR THESE TIMES

WRITTEN BY

ONE OF HIS OWN SERVANTS, BEING HIS GENTLEMAN USHER

EDITED BY

GRACE H. M. SIMPSON

R. & T. WASHBOURNE
18 PATERNOSTER ROW, LONDON
BENZIGER BROS.: NEW YORK, CINCINNATI, AND CHICAGO
1901
[*All rights reserved*]

PREFACE TO THE PRESENT EDITION (1901)

THE author of this book, Sir William Cavendish, was Privy Counsellor during the successive reigns of Henry VIII., Edward VI., and Queen Mary. Preserving to the last great esteem and reverence for his old master, Cardinal Wolsey, he wrote his life.

For a long time it remained only in manuscript, and is quoted by Lord Herbert in his 'History of Henry VIII.,' and by Burnet in his 'History of the Reformation.' It was at length printed for Dorman Newman, and dedicated to the Marquis of Dorset, in 1667. This is the first edition.

I give below a short account of Sir William Cavendish, taken from the 'Biographia Britannica,' published 1748:

'William Cavendish, a great favourite and Privy Counsellor of three Princes, viz., Henry VIII., Edward VI., and Queen Mary, was the second son of Thomas Cavendish, of Cavendish, in the county of Suffolk, Clerk of the Pipe in the reign of Henry VIII., and was born about the year 1505, being descended of very ancient and honourable families, both by his father and mother, as appears by unquestionable authorities. He had a liberal education given him by his father, who settled upon him also certain lands in the county of Suffolk, but made a much better provision for him by procuring him to be admitted into the family of the great Cardinal Wolsey, upon whose person he waited in quality of Gentleman Usher of his chamber at a time when he lived with all the state and dignity of a Prince. . . . As Mr. Cavendish was the Cardinal's countryman, and as he had a great kindness for his father, he took him early into his confidence, and showed him, upon all occasions, very particular marks of kindness and respect.

'In 1527 he attended his master in his splendid embassy to France. . . . He returned with that great Prelate into England, and served him with the utmost zeal and fidelity as well in his disgrace as when in the highest favour, and was one of the few servants that stuck close to him when he had neither office nor salary to bestow upon them. This was so far from prejudicing him in the opinion of his Sovereign, that on this very account he took particular notice of him, and gave him singular intimations of his grace and favour; and after the Cardinal's death, upon whom Mr. Cavendish waited to the last and delayed going to Court till he had seen his body interred, the King took him into his own family and service. He was also constituted one of the Commissioners for visiting and taking the surrenders of several religious houses, and in 1531 he took several surrenders in that capacity. In 1540 he was appointed one of the auditors of the Court of Augmentation, and soon after had a very considerable grant made him of several lordships in the county of Hereford. In 1546 he was made Treasurer of the Chamber to His Majesty, and on Easter Day the same year he had the honour of Knighthood conferred upon him, and was soon after sworn of the Privy Council. He continued to enjoy both these honours for the space of eleven years, in which time his estate was much increased by the grants he received from King Edward VI. in several counties; nor does it appear that he was less in credit or favour with Queen Mary, under whose reign he died, 1557. He married three wives. . . . His third and last wife survived him. By her he had issué three sons and as many daughters. . . .

'He appears from his writings to have been a man of great honour and integrity, a good subject to his Prince, a true lover of his country, and one who preserved to the last a very high reverence and esteem for his old master and first patron, Cardinal Wolsey.'

THE EPISTLE DEDICATORY

TO

THE RIGHT HONOURABLE HENRY,
LORD MARQUIS OF DORCHESTER

MY NOBLE LORD,

True nobility and learning are the grand accomplishments which make your Honour outshine the most of your degree in the cynosure of all arts and sciences, of which your Lordship is so great a master and patron that you despise not the addresses of the meanest endeavours.

My Lord, I have now presumed to dedicate to your Lordship the Life and Death of that famous Cardinal Wolsey, newly reprinted; the subject whereof takes in the most remarkable occurrences of those times, not unworthy the perusal of ours, seeing it is no small advantage future times reap from former ages, and great men from their predecessors; for they may inform themselves what made them shine, to provoke their imitation, and what it was that clouded them, to excite their caution.

My Lord, this great person was then looked upon as the most able pilot to steer things aright, both in Church and State, whilst he was embarked in those two great offices of Lord High Chancellor of England, and Archbishop of York; and so equally did he balance things in those troublesome times that one observes of him, 'That he never spake a word too much, and but one too little'; nor were his successes inconsiderable in begetting a right understanding between foreign nations and home; as in the Netherlands, so especially in France, which he did with so much amity, as if he would cross that pleasant proverb, 'Kingdoms are never married.'

My Lord, had this Cardinal been a man of no conscience (as some would have it), his Honour might have been more lasting; though we have reason to believe his own words (notwithstanding his great magnificence), *i.e.*, that had he been as faithful to his Maker as to his master, he had not been deserted in his old age, when Fortune frowned on him; though, indeed, he died rather neglected than quite cast off.

My Lord, great men are set in the world like diamonds in a ring, and the first thing the vulgar look at is to observe their flaws; which made them think the Cardinal's prosperity might have been more durable, had it been more moderate; but Rickets-like, growing too big in the head, it enfeebled its supporters, yet not so much as to make his own magnificence or memory to be forgotten.

May it therefore please your Honour to countenance this new edition, since the old one hath survived his greatest enemies, and now hath expired, Phœnix-like, to give place to this. I beg your Lordship's pardon for my bold attempt, and disturbing your serious affairs. And that your Lordship may long live, to shine in our English orb, is the prayer of

Your Lordship's most humble servant,
N. D.

AN ADVERTISEMENT TO THE READER

WHO pleaseth to read this history advisedly may well perceive the mutability of honour, the tottering state of earthly dignity, the deceit of flattering friends, and the instability of Princes' favours.

This great Cardinal having experience of all this, witness his fleeting from honour, the loss of friends, riches, dignities, being forgotten of his Prince, whilst Fortune smiled; having satiety of all these, and she bending her brow, deprived him of all terrestrial joys, who by twenty years' study and pains had obtained so great wealth and dignity and in less than one year lost all.

And thus was his honour laid in the dust.

THE PREFACE

IT seemeth no wisdom to credit every light tale, blazed about in the mouths of vulgars, for we daily hear how with their blasphemous trump they spread abroad innumerable lies, without either shame or honesty; which *primâ facie* sheweth forth a visage of truth, as though it were an absolute verity, though indeed nothing less, and amongst the better sort those babblings are of no validity.

I have read the allegations of divers worthy authors against such false rumours and opinions of the common people, who delight in nothing more than to hear strange things and to see new alterations of authority, rejoicing sometimes in such novelties, which afterwards do produce repentance. Thus may all men of understanding conceive the madness of the rude multitude, and not give too much credence to every sudden rumour, until the truth be perfectly known, by the report of some approved and credible persons, that commonly have the best intelligence. I have heard, and also seen set forth in divers printed books, some untrue imaginations, after the death of divers persons (who in their lives were in great estimation), invented rather to bring their honest names in question than otherwise.

Now I intend to write here some special proceedings of Cardinal Wolsey, the great Archbishop, his ascending into honour and great promotion, his continuance in it and sudden falling from the same, a great part whereof shall be of mine own knowledge and some part from credible persons' informations. This Cardinal was my Lord and master, whom in his lifetime I served and so remained with him in his fall continually, during the time of all his troubles, both in the south and north parts until he died.

In all which time I punctually observed all his demeanours, as also in his great triumph and glorious estate. And since his departure, I have heard divers surmised and imagined tales concerning his proceedings and dealings, which I myself have certainly known to be most untrue, unto which I could have sufficiently answered according to truth; but conceiving it to be much better to be silent than to reply against their untruths, whereby I might perhaps have rather kindled a great flame of displeasure than have quenched one spark of their untrue reports, therefore I did refer the truth thereof to the Almighty, Who knows the truth of all things.

Nevertheless, whatsoever any man hath conceived of him in his life or since his death, thus much I dare say without offence to any, that in my judgment I never saw this realm in better obedience and quiet than it was in the time of his authority, nor justice better administered without partiality, as I could justly prove, if I should not be taxed with too much affection.

I will therefore here desist to speak any further by the way of apology, and proceed now to speak of his origin and of ascending through fortune's favour to high dignity and abundance of wealth.

CONTENTS

CHAPTER	PAGE
I. OF THE CARDINAL'S ORIGIN, AND WHO HE WAS	19
II. OF THE CARDINAL'S SPEEDY DESPATCH IN HIS FIRST AMBASSAGE TO THE EMPEROR MAXIMILIAN	25
III. OF KING HENRY'S INVADING FRANCE IN HIS OWN PERSON, WITH THE CARDINAL'S ASSISTANCE	31
IV. THE KING PROMOTING HIS ALMONER, WOLSEY BEING MADE CARDINAL AND LORD CHANCELLOR OF ENGLAND	35
V. OF THE ORDERS AND OFFICES OF HIS HOUSE AND CHAPEL	38
VI. OF HIS SECOND AMBASSAGE TO THE EMPEROR CHARLES V.	43
VII. OF THE MANNER OF HIS GOING TO WESTMINSTER HALL	46
VIII. OF THE CARDINAL'S MAGNIFICENCE IN HIS HOUSE	49
IX. OF THE ORIGINAL INSTRUMENT OF THE CARDINAL'S FALL, MISTRESS ANNE BOLEYN	55
X. OF MISTRESS ANNE BOLEYN'S FAVOUR WITH THE KING	59
XI. OF THE VARIANCE BETWEEN THE FRENCH KING AND THE DUKE OF BOURBON, ETC.	63
XII. OF THE DUKE OF BOURBON'S STRATAGEM AND VICTORY, WHEREIN THE FRENCH KING WAS TAKEN PRISONER	67

CONTENTS

CHAPTER		PAGE
XIII.	OF THE FRENCH KING'S REDEMPTION OUT OF CAPTIVITY, AND OF THE CARDINAL'S AMBASSAGE INTO FRANCE	73
XIV.	OF THE FRENCH AMBASSADOR'S ENTERTAINMENT AND DESPATCH	100
XV.	OF THE KING'S DISCOVERY OF HIS LOVE FOR MISTRESS ANNE BOLEYN TO THE CARDINAL, WITH THE CARDINAL'S DISLIKE, ETC.	112
XVI.	A NEW COURT ERECTED TO DETERMINE THE KING'S CASE, TWO CARDINALS BEING JUDGES, AND OF THE ISSUE	118
XVII.	OF CERTAIN PASSAGES CONDUCING TO THE CARDINAL'S FALL	136
XVIII.	THE CARDINAL ACCUSED OF HIGH TREASON IN THE PARLIAMENT HOUSE, AND MR. CROMWELL'S DEFENCE FOR HIM	149
XIX.	OF THE CARDINAL'S FALL, AND HOW HE WAS ARRESTED OF HIGH TREASON	169
XX.	OF THE CARDINAL'S ENTERTAINMENT AT THE EARL OF SHREWSBURY'S, AND OF HIS DEATH AND BURIAL	179

LIFE OF CARDINAL WOLSEY

I

OF THE CARDINAL'S ORIGIN, AND WHO HE WAS

TRUTH it is Cardinal Wolsey was an honest poor man's son in the town of Ipswich, in the county of Suffolk, and there born, who, being but a child, was very apt to learn, wherefore, by means of his parents and other good friends, he was maintained at the University of Oxford, where in a short time he prospered so well, that in a small time (as he told me with his own mouth) he was made Batchelor of Arts, when he was but fifteen years of age, and was most commonly called the 'Boy Batchelor.' Thus prospering in learning, he was made Fellow of Magdalen College in Oxford; after that he was made Master of Magdalen School, at which time there were the Lord Marquis of Dorset's sons there at school, committing unto him as well their education as their instructions and learning.

It pleased this Lord Marquis against Christmas to send as well for the schoolmaster as for the scholars home to his house, for their recreation in that pleasant and honourable forest. They being awhile there, the Lord Marquis, their father, perceiving them to be well improved in learning for the time, he was so well contented, that he having a benefice in his gift (being at that present void), gave the schoolmaster the same in regard of his diligence. After Christmas, at his departure to the University, and he having the presentation thereof, repaired to the Ordinary for his institution, and being then furnished with all his instruments at the Ordinary's hands for his preferment, made haste without any further delay to his benefice to take possession thereof. Now you shall understand that the schoolmaster had not been long there, but one Sir James Pawlet, Knight, dwelling in the country thereabouts, took an occasion of displeasure against him, but upon what ground I know not, insomuch that Sir James was so bold as to set the schoolmaster by the heels during his displeasure, which affront was afterwards neither forgotten nor forgiven; for when the schoolmaster mounted so high as to be Lord Chancellor of England, he was not forgetful of his old dis-

THE CARDINAL'S ORIGIN, AND WHO HE WAS 21

pleasure, most cruelly ministered unto him by Sir James, but sent for him, and after a very sharp reproof, enjoined him not to depart out of London without license first obtained, so that he continued in the Middle Temple the space of five or six years, who afterwards lay in the Gate-House next the stairs, which he re-edified and sumptuously beautified the same all over on the outside with the Cardinal's arms, his hat, his cognizance and badges, with other devices in so glorious a manner, as he thought thereby to have appeased his old displeasure. This may be a good precedent for men in authority, which work their own wills without wit, to remember that greatness may decay. And those whom they do punish more of humour than justice may afterwards be advanced to great honour (as this Cardinal was), and they abased as low as this Sir James was, which seek revenge.

Who would have thought that when Sir James Pawlet punished this poor schoolmaster that ever he should have mounted to so great dignity as to be Chancellor of England, considering his mean parentage and friends? These be the most wonderful works of God's providence, and I would that all men in authority would fear God in all ages in the time of their triumph and greatness, considering that advancement and authority are not permanent, but many times slide and vanish suddenly away, as Princes' pleasures alter and change, or as all living creatures must of necessity pay the debt due to Nature, which no earthly creature can resist.

Shortly after it chanced the said Lord Marquis died, after whose decease the schoolmaster, thinking himself but a weak beneficed man, and that he had left his Fellowship in the College, for (as I understand) if a Fellow of that House be once promoted to a Benefice, he shall by the rules of the same house be dismissed of his Fellowship; and now being also destitute of his singular good Lord as well as of his Fellowship, which was most of his relief, though long to be provided of some other help to defend him from all such storms as he might meet with. In his travel thereabouts he grew acquainted with a very great and ancient knight who had a great place at Calais under Henry VII. This knight he served and behaved himself so discreetly that he obtained the special favour of his said master, insomuch that for his wit and gravity he committed all the care and charge of his said office to his said Chaplain. And as I understand, his office was the Treasurership of Calais, who in regard of his great age shortly after was discharged of his said Office, and so returned into England, intending to live a more private life. But through his instant labour and good favour his Chaplain was preferred to be the King's Chaplain. And when he had once cast anchor in the port of promotion, how he then bestirred himself I shall now declare. He having then just occasion to be daily in sight of the King in his Closet, not spending the rest of the day in idleness, would attend those men whom he thought to bear most rule in the Council, and were most in favour with the King, which at that time was Doctor Fox, Bishop of Winchester, and Lord Privy Seal, and also Sir Thomas Lovell, Knight, a very sage and wise Counsellor, being Master of the Wards, and Constable of the Tower. These ancient and grave Counsellors in process of time, perceiving this Chaplain to be a man of a very acute wit, thought him a meet instrument to be employed in greater affairs.

Not long after it happened that the King had an urgent occasion to send an Ambassador to Maximilian, the Emperor, who lay at that present in the Low Countries at Flanders, and not far from Calais.

Now, the Bishop of Winchester and Sir Thomas Lovell, whom the King most esteemed as the chiefest of his Council, one day were advising and debating with themselves upon this ambassage, and by this time they saw they had a convenient occasion to prefer the King's Chaplain, whose excellent eloquence and learning they highly commended unto the King's Highness, who giving ear unto them and being a Prince of an excellent judgment and modesty, he commanded them to bring his Chaplain (whom they so commended) before his Grace; and being come, His Majesty (to prove his ability) entered into discourse with him concerning matters of State, whereby the King had so well informed himself, that he found him to be a man of a sharp wit and such excellent parts, that he thought him worthy to be put in trust with matters of greater consequence.

II

OF THE CARDINAL'S SPEEDY DESPATCH IN HIS FIRST AMBASSAGE TO THE EMPEROR MAXIMILIAN

THE King, being now resolved to employ him in this ambassage, commanded him thereupon to prepare himself for his journey, and for his despatch, wished him to repair to his Grace and his Council, of whom he should receive his commission and instruction, by means whereof he had then a fit occasion to repair from time to time into the King's presence, who had thereby daily experience of his singular wisdom and sound judgment. Thus, having his despatch, he took his leave of the King at Richmond, about four of the clock in the afternoon. He launched forth in a Gravesend barge with a prosperous wind and tide, and his happy speed was such that he arrived at Gravesend in little more than three hours, where he tarried no longer than the post-horses were provided; and he travelled so speedily that he came to Dover the next morning, where the passengers were under sail to pass to Calais, so that long before noon he arrived there. Having post-horses prepared, he departed from thence without tarrying, making such hasty speed that he was that night with the Emperor, who, understanding of the arrival of the King of England's Ambassador, would in no wise delay time, but sent for him immediately, for his affection for the King of England was such that he was glad of any opportunity to do him a courtesy.

The Ambassador declared the sum of his embassy unto the Emperor, of whom he craved speedy expedition, which was granted him, so that next day he was clearly despatched, and all the King's requests fully accomplished and granted. At which time he made no further stay, but took post-horses that night, and rode without intermission to Calais, being conducted thither by divers nobles appointed by the Emperor. At the opening of the gates of Calais, he came thither where the passengers were ready to return to England, insomuch that he arrived at Dover between ten and eleven of the clock in the forenoon.

Having post-horses in readiness, he came to the

Court at Richmond that same night, where, taking his repose until morning, he presented himself unto His Majesty at his first coming out of his bedchamber to his Closet to Mass, whom when he saw he checked for that he was not in his journey.

'Sir,' quoth he, 'if it may please your Highness, I have already been with the Emperor and despatched your affairs, I trust, to your Grace's content;' and thereupon presented the King with his letters of credence from the Emperor.

The King, wondering at his speedy return (he being so well furnished with all his proceedings), for the present dissembled his admiration and imagination in that matter, and demanded of him whether he encountered with his pursuivant, which he sent unto him with letters (imagining him to be scarce out of London), which concerned very material passages which were omitted in their consultation, which the King earnestly desired should have been despatched in his ambassage.

'Yes, forsooth,' quoth he, 'I met with him yesterday by the way, and though I had no knowledge thereof, yet notwithstanding I have been so bold (upon mine own discretion), perceiving the matter to be very necessary, in that behalf I despatched the same. And forasmuch as I have been so bold to exceed my commission, I most humbly crave your royal remission and pardon.'

The King, inwardly rejoicing, replied:

'We do not only pardon you, but give you our princely thanks, both for your good exploit and happy expedition.'

He then dismissed him for that present, and bade him return to him again after dinner for a further relation of his ambassage; and so the King went to Mass.

It is not to be doubted but this Ambassador had all this while visited his great friends, the Bishop of Winchester and Sir Thomas Lovell, to whom he had declared the effect of his ambassage; and also His Majesty's commendations did not a little rejoice the worthy Counsellors, forasmuch as he was of their preferment. And shortly after the King gave him for his diligent service the Deanery of Lincoln, which was in those days one of the greatest promotions that he gave under the degree of a Bishop. He grew more and more in estimation and authority, and was afterwards promoted to be Almoner.

Now, not long after, when Death (that favoureth no estates, nor King, nor Emperor) had taken away the wife of King Henry VII. out of this present life, it was a wonder to see what practices and devices were then used about the young Prince, Henry VIII.; the great provision that was then made for the funeral of the one and for the Coronation of the other by the now Queen Katherine and mother, after the Queen's Highness that now is, whose virtuous life Jesu long preserve.

After the solemnizations and costly triumphs, our natural, young, courageous, lusty Prince and Sovereign Lord, King Henry VIII., entering into his flower and lusty youth, took upon him the royal sceptre and imperial diadem of this fertile nation, the two and twentieth of April, A.D. 1509, which at that time flourished with all abundance of riches, whereof the King was most inestimably furnished, called them the golden world. Now, shortly after, the Almoner, seeing he had a plain pathway to promotion, behaved himself so politicly that he was made one of the King's Privy Council, and increased in favour daily: to whom he gave a house at Bridewell, near Fleet Street, where he kept his house for his family, and so he daily attended upon the King, being in special favour.

His sentences in the Star Chamber were ever so pithy and witty, that upon all occasions they assigned him, for the fluent eloquence of his tongue, to be Expositor to the King in all their proceedings. In whom the King conceived so great content that he called him still nearer to his person; and the rather because he was ready to advance the King's own will and pleasure, having no respect to the case.

Now, the King being young and much given to his pleasure, his old Counsellors advised him to have recourse sometimes to the Council about his weighty affairs; but the Almoner, on the contrary, persuaded him to mind his pleasure, and he would take his care and charge upon himself (if His Majesty would countenance him with his authority), which the King liked well. And thus none was like to the Almoner in favour with the King.

III

OF KING HENRY'S INVADING FRANCE IN HIS OWN PERSON, WITH THE CARDINAL'S ASSISTANCE

THUS the Almoner, continuing in high favour, till at last many presents, gifts and rewards came in so plentifully that I dare say he wanted nothing, for he had all things in abundance that might either please his fancy or enrich his coffers, for the times so favourably smiled upon him, but to what end you shall hereafter hear. Therefore let all men to whom Fortune extendeth her favour and grace take heed they trust not her subtle and fair promises, for under colour thereof she carrieth an envious gall; for when she seeth her servant in highest authority she turneth her favour and pleasant countenance into frowns.

This Almoner climbed up Fortune's wheel so that no man was in estimation with the King but only he, for his witty qualities and wisdom. He had an especial gift of natural eloquence and a ready tongue to pronounce the same, so that he was able therewith to persuade and allure all men to his purposes in the time of his continuance in Fortune's favour.

In the fifth year of the reign of King Henry VIII. it chanced that the realms of England and France were at variance, but upon what ground or occasion I know not, insomuch that the King was fully resolved in his own person to invade France with a powerful army. It was therefore thought very necessary that his royal enterprises should be speedily provided and furnished in every degree in things apt and convenient for the same.

For expedition the King thought no man's wit so meet for policy and painful travel as the Almoner, to whom he committed his whole confidence and trust therein. The Almoner, being nothing scrupulous in anything that the King would command, although it seemed very difficult, took upon him the whole charge of the business, and proceeded so therein that he brought all things to good effect in direct order for all manner of victuals and provision convenient for so noble a voyage and army. All things being thus prepared by him in order, the King not intending to neglect or delay any time, but with noble and valiant courage to advance his royal enterprise, passed the seas between Dover and Calais, where he prosperously arrived. And after he had there made his arrival, and landed all his provision and munition and sate in consultation about his weighty affairs, he marched forth in good order of battle till he came to the strong town of Terouanne, to the which he laid strong siege and made a sharp assault, so that in short space it was yielded unto him, unto which place the Emperor Maximilian resorted unto him with a great army, like a mighty Prince taking off the King's wages.

Thus, after the King had taken this strong town, and taken possession thereof, and set all things in good order for the defence and preservation thereof to His Majesty's use, then he retired from thence, and marched towards Tournay, and there laid siege in like manner, to which he gave so fierce assault that the enemies were constrained to surrender the town to His Majesty, at which time the King gave unto the Almoner the Bishopric of the same see for his pains and diligence shown in that journey. And when he had established all things according to his princely mind and pleasure, and the same with men and captains of war for the safeguard of the town, he prepared for his return to England.

But now you shall understand by the way that whilst the King was absent with a great power in

France, the Scottish King invaded England, against whom the Queen sent a great army, the Earl of Surrey being General. The Scots were overthrown at Balmston, called Hoddenfield, where the King of Scots was slain with divers of his nobility and 18,000 men, and they took all his munition for war.

By this time the King returned into England, and took with him divers noble personages of France, being prisoners, as the Duke of Longuido, Viscount Clerimond, with divers others that were taken in a skirmish.

And thus God gave him victory at home and victory abroad, being in the fifth year of his reign, A.D. 1513.

IV

THE KING PROMOTING HIS ALMONER, WOLSEY BEING MADE CARDINAL AND LORD CHANCELLOR OF ENGLAND

THE King being returned into England, the See of Lincoln became void by the death of Doctor Smith, late Bishop there, which Bishopric the King gave to his Almoner, the Bishop Elect of Tournay, who was not negligent to take possession thereof, but made all speed for his consecration. The solemnization thereof being ended, he found a way to get into his hands all his predecessor's goods, whereof I have seen divers parts that furnished his house.

It was not long after but Doctor Bambridge, Archbishop of York, died at Rouen in France, being there the King's ambassador. Unto this See the King presented the last new Bishop of Lincoln, so that he had three Bishoprics in his hands at one time, all in one year given him.

Then prepared he again for his translation from the See of Lincoln to that of York, as he did before to his installation.

After which solemnization done, and being then Archbishop and Primus Angliæ, he thought himself sufficient to compare with that of Canterbury, and did thereupon erect his Crosses in the Courts and every other place, as well in the precinct and jurisdiction of Canterbury as any other place.

And though Canterbury claimeth a superiority over York as well as over any other bishopric within England, and for that cause claimeth an acknowledgment as in ancient obedience of York, to abate advancement of his Cross in the presence of the Cross of Canterbury, notwithstanding, York did not desist to bear the same, although Canterbury gave York a check for the same and told him it was presumption, by reason whereof there engendered some grudge between them. But shortly after he obtained to be made Cardinal and Legatus de Latere, unto whom the Pope sent the Cardinal's Cap and certain Bulls for his authority in that behalf. Whereupon he was installed at Westminster in great triumph, which was executed by all Bishops with their mitres, caps and other ornaments. And after all this he was made Chancellor of England, and Canterbury, who was the Chancellor, was dismissed. Now he being in the Chancellorship and endowed with the promotions of Archbishop and Cardinal de Latere, thought himself so fully furnished that he was now able to surmount Canterbury in all jurisdictions, and in all ecclesiastical powers to convocate Canterbury and all other bishops and spiritual persons to assemble at his Convocations, where he would assign and take upon him the conversion of all ministers and others within their jurisdictions, and visit all the spiritual houses in their Dioceses, and all manner of spiritual ministers as Commissioners, Scribes, Apparitors and all other necessary Officers to furnish his Courts, and did present benefices to whom he pleased through this realm and dominion and all other persons to the glory of his dignity. Then had he two great Crosses of silver, whereof one was of his Archbishopric and the other of his Legacy, borne before him wheresoever he rode or went, by two of the tallest priests that he could get in this realm.

And to the increase of his gain, he had in his hand the Bishopric of Durham and St. Albans 'in commendam.' Also when Doctor Fox, Bishop of Winchester, died, he did surrender Durham to the King and took himself to Winchester. He had also, as it were in farm, the Bishoprics of Bath, Worcester and Hereford, for the incumbents of them were foreigners. He had also attending upon him men of great possessions and the tallest yeomen for his guard in the realm.

V

OF THE ORDERS AND OFFICES OF HIS HOUSE AND CHAPEL

NOW, first for his house. You shall understand that he had in his hall three boards kept with three several officers—that is to say, a Steward (that was always a priest); a Treasurer (that was ever a Knight); and a Controller (that was an Esquire); also a Confessor, a Doctor, three Marshals, three Ushers in the hall, besides two Almoners and Grooms.

Then he had in the hall-kitchen two clerks—a Clerk Comptroller and a Surveyor over the dresser; a clerk in the spicery, which kept continually a mess together in the hall; also he had in the hall-kitchen two cooks and labourers and children, twelve persons, four men of the scullery, two Yeomen of the Pantry, with two other paste-layers under the yeomen.

Then had he in his kitchen a master-cook, who

went daily in velvet or satin, with a gold chain, besides two other cooks and six labourers in the same room. In the larder, one yeoman and a groom; in the scullery, one yeoman and two grooms; in the buttery, two yeomen and two grooms; in the ewery, so many; in the cellar, three yeomen, three pages; in the chandlery, two yeomen; in the wayfary, two yeomen; in the wardrobe of beds, the Master of the Wardrobe and twenty persons besides; in the laundry, a yeoman and a groom and thirteen pages, two yeomen-purveyors and a groom-purveyor; in the bakehouse, two yeomen and grooms; in the wood-yard, one yeoman and a groom; in the barn, one yeoman; porters at the gate, two yeomen and two grooms; a yeoman in his barge and a Master of his Horse; a clerk of the stables and a yeoman of the same; a farrier, and a Yeoman of the Stirrup; a muleteer and sixteen grooms, every one of them keeping four geldings.

Now will I declare unto you the officers of his chapel and singing-men of the same.

First, he had there a Dean, a great divine and a man of excellent learning; and a Sub-Dean, a Repeater of the Choir, a Gospeller, an Epistoler of the Singing Priests, a Master of the Children; in the vestry a yeoman and two grooms, besides other retainers that came thither at principal Feasts.

And for the furniture of his chapel, it passeth my weak capacity to declare the number of the costly ornaments and rich jewels that were occupied in the same; for I have seen in procession about the hall forty-four rich copes of one suit very rich, besides the rich candlesticks and other necessary ornaments to the furniture of the same.

Now you shall understand that he had two cross-bearers and two pillar-bearers in his great chamber, and in his privy chamber all these persons: the Chief Chamberlain, a Vice-Chamberlain, a Gentleman Usher, beside one of his privy chamber; he had also twelve waiters and six gentlemen waiters; also he had nine or ten Lords, who had each of them two or three men to wait upon him, except the Earl of Derby, who had five men.

Then he had of gentlemen, cup-bearers and carvers, sewers, both of the great chamber and of the privy chamber, forty persons, six Yeomen Ushers, eight Grooms of his Chamber; also he had of alms (who were daily waiters of his board at dinner), twelve doctors and chaplains besides them of his which I have rehearsed; a Clerk of his Closet and two Secretaries, and two Clerks of his Signet; four Counsellors learned in the law.

And for that he was Chancellor of England, it

was necessary to have officers of the Chancery to attend him for the better furniture of the same.

First, he had a Riding Clerk, a Clerk of the Crown, a Clerk of the Hamper, a Chaser; then had he a Clerk of the Check, as well upon the chaplains as upon the yeomen of the chamber; he had also four footmen garnished with rich running-coats, whensoever he had any journey.

Then he had a Herald-of-Arms, a Sergeant-of-Arms, a Physician, an Apothecary, four minstrels, a keeper of his tents, an Armourer, an Instructor of his wardrobe of robes, a keeper of his chamber continually.

He had also in his house a Surveyor of York, a Clerk of the Green-cloth. All these were daily attending down-lying and up-rising. And at meat he had eight continual boards for the chamberlains and gentlemen officers, having a mess of young lords and another of gentlemen; besides this, there was never a gentleman or officer or other worthy person, but he kept some two, some three persons to wait upon them, and all others at the least had one, which did amount to a great number of persons.

Now, I have declared the order according to the chain-roll of his house and what officers he had daily attending to furnish the same; besides, retainers and other persons being suitors dined in the hall.

And when shall we see any more such subjects that shall keep such a noble house? Therefore here is an end of his household; the number of persons in the chain-roll were eight hundred persons.

VI

OF HIS SECOND AMBASSAGE TO THE EMPEROR CHARLES V.

WHEN he was furnished in manner as I have before rehearsed unto you, he was sent twice on ambassage to the Emperor Charles V., that now reigneth, and father to King Philip, now our Lord and Sovereign.

Forasmuch as the old Emperor Maximilian was dead, and for divers other urgent occasions touching His Majesty, it was thought fit that, about such weighty matters and so noble a Prince, the Cardinal was most meet to be sent on this ambassage, and he, being one ready to take the charge thereof upon him, was furnished in every respect most like a great Prince, which was much to the honour of His Majesty and of this realm. For first he proceeded forth like to a Cardinal, having all things correspondent; his gentlemen, being very many in number, were clothed in livery coats of crimson velvet of the best and chains of gold about their necks, and his yeomen and all his mean officers were clad in fine scarlet, guarded with black velvet one hand breadth. Thus furnished, he was twice sent in this manner to the Emperor in Flanders, then lying at Bruges, whom he did most nobly entertain, discharging all his own charges and his men's. There was no house in the town of Bruges wherein any one of my Lord's gentlemen were lodged or had recourse but that the owners of the houses were commanded by the Emperor's officers, upon pain of their lives, to take no money for anything that the Cardinal's men did take of any kind of victuals. No, although they were disposed to make costly banquets, further commanding their said hosts that they should want nothing which they honestly required or desired to have.

Also the Emperor's officers every night went through the town from house to house, where any English had recourse or lodged, and served their livery for all night, which was done on this manner. First, the officers brought into the house of Castille a fine manchet, then two silver pots of wine and a pound of sugar, white lights and yellow lights, a bowl of silver and a goblet to drink in, and every night a staff torch. This was their order of their livery every night; and in the morning, when the officers came to fetch away their stuff, they would account for the gentlemen's costs the day before.

Thus the Emperor entertained the Cardinal and his train during the time of their embassy. And that done, he returned into England with great triumph, being no less in estimation with the King than he was before, but rather much more, for he increased daily in the King's favour, by reason of wits and readiness to do the King's pleasure in all things. In the one and twentieth year of King Henry VIII.'s reign, A.D. 1529, this Emperor Charles V. came into England, who was nobly entertained.

VII

OF THE MANNER OF HIS GOING TO WEST-MINSTER HALL

NOW I must declare the manner of his going to Westminster Hall in the Term time. First, when he came out of his Privy Chamber he most commonly heard two Masses in his Chapel or Chamber. And I heard one of his Chaplains say since (that was a man of credit and excellent learning) that what business soever the Cardinal had in the daytime, that he never went to bed with any part of his service unsaid—no, not so much as one Collect, in which I think he deceived many a man. Then, going into his chamber again, he demanded of some of his servants if they were in readiness and had furnished his Chamber of Presence and Waiting Chamber; he, being then advertised, came out of his Privy Chamber about eight of the clock, ready apparelled and in red like a Cardinal; his upper vesture was all of scarlet or else of fine crimson taffeta or crimson satin engrained, his pillion of scarlet, with a black velvet tippet of sables about his neck, holding in his hand an orange, the meat or substance thereof being taken out and filled again with a piece of sponge, with vinegar and other confections against pestilent airs, the which he most commonly held to his nose when he came to the presses, or when he was pestered with many suitors. Before him was borne the Broad Seal of England and the Cardinal's hat by some Lord or some gentleman of worship right solemnly, and as soon as he was entered into his Chamber of Presence, where there were daily attending on him, as well noble men of this realm as other worthy gentlemen of his own family, his two great Crosses were there preceding him. Then cried the Gentlemen Ushers, that went before him bareheaded: 'On, masters, before, and make room for my Lord!' Thus went he down into the hall, with a Sergeant-of-Arms before him bearing a great mace of silver and two gentlemen carrying two great plates of silver, and when he came to the door there his mule stood trapped all in crimson velvet, with a saddle of the same.

Then was attending him, when he was mounted, his two cross-bearers, his two pillar-bearers, all upon great horses, all in fine scarlet; then he marched on with a train of gentry, having four footmen about him, bearing every one of them a poleaxe in his hand. Thus he passed forth till he came to Westminster, and there alighted and went in this manner up to the Chancery and stayed awhile at the Bar, made for him beneath the Chancery, and there he communed sometimes with judges and sometimes with other persons, and then went up to the Chancery and sat there till eleven of the clock to hear suits and to determine causes. From thence he would go into the Star Chamber as occasion served him; he neither spared high nor low, but did judge everyone according unto right.

Every Sunday he would resort to the Court being at Greenwich with his former rehearsed train and triumph, taking his barge at his own stairs, furnished with yeomen standing upon the sails and his gentlemen within and about, and landed at the Three Cranes in the Vine Tree, and from thence he rode upon his mule with his crosses, his pillars, his hat, and his broad seal carried before him on horseback along Thames Street until he came to Billingsgate, and there he took his barge and so went to Greenwich, where he was nobly entertained of the Lords in the King's house, being there with staves in their hands as the Treasurer, Comptroller, with many others. He was conveyed into the King's chamber, and so went home again in the like triumph.

VIII

OF THE CARDINAL'S MAGNIFICENCE IN HIS HOUSE

HE lived a long season, ruling all things in this realm appertaining to the King by his wisdom and all other matters of foreign regions, with whom the King had any occasion to meddle. All ambassadors of foreign Potentates were ever disposed by the Cardinal's wisdom, to whom they had continual access for their despatch. His house was always resorted unto like a King's house by noblemen and gentlemen, and when it pleased the King's Majesty (as many times it did), he would for his recreation resort unto the Cardinal's house, against whose coming there wanted no preparation of goodly furniture, with victuals of the finest sort that could be had for money or friendship.

Such pleasures were here devised for the King's delight as could be invented or imagined ; banquets set with maskers and mummers in such costly manner that it was glorious to behold; there wanted no damsels meet to dance with the maskers, or to garnish the place for the time with variety of other pastimes. Then was there divers kinds of music, and many choice men and women singers appointed to sing who had excellent voices. I have seen the King come suddenly thither in a mask with a dozen maskers all in garments like shepherds, made of fine cloth of gold and silver wire and six torch-bearers, besides their drummers and others attending on them with vizards, and clothed in satin. And before his entering into the Hall, you shall understand, that he came by water up to the water-gate without any noise, where were laid divers chambers and guns charged with shot, and at his landing they were discharged, which made such a rattling noise in the air that it was like thunder. It made all the noblemen, gentlemen and ladies to muse what it should mean coming so suddenly, they sitting quietly at a banquet. In this sort you shall understand that the tables were set in the Chamber of Presence, and my Lord Cardinal sitting under his cloth of State, and there having all his service alone; and then was there set a lady and a nobleman, a gentleman and a gentlewoman throughout all the tables in the chambers on the one side, which were made all joining, as it were, but one table. All which order was done by my Lord Sands, then Lord Chamberlain to the King, and by Sir Henry Guildford, then Comptroller of the King's house.

Then, immediately after this great shot of guns, the Cardinal desired the Lord Chamberlain to see what it did mean, as though he knew nothing of the matter. They then looked out of the window into the Thames, and returning again, told him that they thought they were noblemen and strangers arrived at the bridge, and coming as ambassadors from some foreign Prince.

With that said the Cardinal:

'I desire you, because you can speak French, to take pains to go into the hall, there to receive them into the chamber, where they shall see us and all those noble personages being merry at our banquet, desiring them to sit down with us and take part of our fare.'

Then went they directly into the hall, where they were received with twenty torches and conveyed up into the chamber, with such a number of drums and flutes as I have seldom seen together at one time and place.

Then, at their arrival into the chamber, they went two and two together directly before the Cardinal where he sat and saluted them very reverently, to whom the Lord Chamberlain for them said :

'Sir, forasmuch as they are strangers and cannot speak English, they have desired me to declare unto you that they having understanding of this your triumphant banquet, at which were assembled such a number of fair dames, they could do no less (under the support of your Grace) than to view as well their incomparable beauties, as to accompany them to the "mumchance," and after that to dance with them, so to beget their better acquaintance. And, furthermore, they require of your Grace licence to accomplish this cause of their coming.'

Then the Cardinal said he was willing and very well content they should do so.

Then went the maskers and first saluted all the dames, and then returned to the most worthiest, and there opened the great cup of gold filled with crowns and other pieces to cast with.

Thus perusing all the gentlewomen, of some they won and of some they lost. And having viewed all the ladies, they returned to the Cardinal, with great reverence, pouring down all their gold, which was above two hundred crowns.

'At all,' quoth the Cardinal, and casting the die, he won it, whereat was made great joy.

Then quoth the Cardinal to my Lord Chamberlain:

'I pray you go tell them, that to me it seemeth that there should be a noble man amongst them, that better deserves to sit in this place than I, to whom I should gladly surrender the same according to my duty if I knew him.'

Then spake my Lord Chamberlain to them in French, declaring my Lord Cardinal's words, and they rounding* him again in the ear, the Lord Chamberlain said unto my Lord Cardinal:

'Sir,' quoth he, 'they confess that among them is such a noble personage, whom, if your Grace can point out from the rest, he is contented to disclose himself and to accept of your place most willingly.'

With that, the Cardinal, taking good advice, went amongst them, and at the last quoth he, 'It seemeth to me that the gentleman with the black beard should be he,' and with that he rose from out his chair and offered the same to the gentleman with the black beard, with the cup in his hand. But the Cardinal was mistaken, for the person to whom he then offered his chair was Sir Edward Nevil, a comely Knight, and of a goodly personage, who did more resemble His Majesty's person than any other in that mask.

* 'Rounding,' sometimes spelt 'rowning,' *i.e.* 'whispering.'

The King seeing the Cardinal so deceived in his choice, could not forbear laughing, but pulled down his vizard and Sir Edward Nevil's also, with such a pleasant countenance and cheer, that all the noblemen desired His Highness to take his place. To whom the King made answer, that he would first go and shift himself; and thereupon went into the Cardinal's bedchamber, where was a great fire prepared for him, and there he new apparelled himself with rich and princely garments. In the King's absence, the dishes of the banquet were clean taken away, and the tables covered again with new and perfumed cloths, every man sitting still until the King's Majesty with his maskers came in among them, every man new apparelled.

Then the King took his seat under the cloth of State, commanding every person to sit still as they did before. And then came in a new banquet before His Majesty of two hundred dishes, and so they passed the night in banqueting and dancing until the morning, and it much rejoiced the Cardinal to see his Sovereign Lord so pleasant at his house.

IX

OF THE ORIGINAL INSTRUMENT OF THE CARDINAL'S FALL, MISTRESS ANNE BOLEYN

NOW you shall understand that the young Lord of Northumberland attended upon my Lord Cardinal, who, when the Cardinal went to Court, would ever have conference with Mistress Anne Boleyn, who then was one of the Maids of Honour to Queen Katherine, insomuch that at last they were contracted together, which, when the King heard, he was much moved thereat (for he had a private affection to her himself, which was not yet discovered to any), and then advised the Cardinal to send for the Earl of Northumberland, his father, and take order to dissolve the contract made between the said parties, which the Lord Cardinal did, after a sharp reprehension, because it was contracted without the King's and his father's knowledge. He sent for his father, who came up to London very speedily, and came first to my Lord Cardinal, as all great personages did that in such sort were sent for, of whom they were advertised of the cause of their sending for. And when the Earl was come, he was presently brought to the Cardinal into the gallery. After whose meeting my Lord Cardinal and he were in secret communication a long space. After their long discourse and drinking a cup of wine, the Earl departed, and at his going away, he sat down at the gallery end in the hall upon a form, and being set, called his son unto him and said: 'Son, even as thou art and ever hast been a proud, disdainful and very unthrifty waster, so hast thou now declared thyself; wherefore what joy, what pleasure, what comfort or what solace can I conceive in thee, that thus without discretion hast abused thyself, having neither regard to me thy natural father, nor unto thy natural Sovereign Lord, to whom all honest and loyal subjects bear faithful obedience, nor yet to the prosperity of thine own estate, but hast so unadvisedly ensnared thyself to her for whom thou hast purchased the King's high displeasure, intolerable for any subject to sustain. And but that the King doth consider the lightness of thy head and wilful qualities of thy person, his displeasure and indignation were sufficient to cast me and all my posterity into utter ruin and destruction. But he being my singular good Lord and favorable Prince, and my Lord Cardinal my very good friend, hath and doth clearly excuse me in thy lewdness, and doth rather lament thy folly than malign thee, and hath advised an order to be taken for thee, to whom both you and I are more bound, than we conceive of. I pray to God that this may be a sufficient admonition unto thee to use thyself more wisely hereafter, for assure thyself that if thou dost not amend thy prodigality, thou wilt be the last Earl of our house. For thy natural inclination, thou art masterful and prodigal, to consume all that thy progenitors have with great travail gathered and kept together with honour. But having the King's Majesty my singular good Lord, I trust (I assure thee) so to order my succession that thou shalt consume thereof but a little. For I do not intend, I tell thee, truly to make thee heir, for, thanks be to God, I have more boys, that I trust will use themselves much better and prove more like to wise and honest men, of whom I will choose the most likely to succeed me.

'Now, good masters and gentlemen,' quoth he to the servants, 'it may be your chances hereafter, when I am dead, to see those things that I have spoken to my son prove as true as I now speak them; yet in the meantime I desire you all to be his friends and tell him his faults, in what he doth amiss, wherein you shall show yourselves friendly to him, and so I take my leave of you; and, son, go your ways unto my Lord and Master and serve him diligently.' And he parted and went down into the hall and so took his barge.

Then after long and large debating the matter about the Lord Percy's assurance to Mistress Anne Boleyn, it was devised that the contract should be infringed and dissolved, and that Lord Percy should marry one of the Earl of Shrewsbury's daughters. And so indeed not long after he did, whereby the former contract was broken and dissolved, wherewith Mistress Anne was greatly displeased, promising that if ever it lay in her power, she would do the Cardinal some displeasure, which she afterwards did. But yet he was not altogether to be blamed, for he did nothing but what the King commanded, whereby the Lord Percy was charged to avoid her company. And so was she for a time discharged at the Court and sent home to her father, whereat she was much troubled and perplexed. For all this time she knew nothing of the King's intended purpose. But we may see when Fortune doth begin to frown how she can compass a matter of displeasure through a far-fetch mark; now therefore of the grudge—how it began that in process of time wrought the Cardinal's utter destruction.

X

OF MISTRESS ANNE BOLEYN'S FAVOUR WITH THE KING

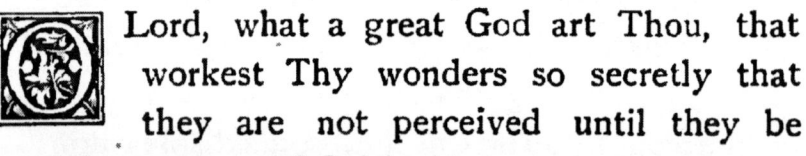

O Lord, what a great God art Thou, that workest Thy wonders so secretly that they are not perceived until they be brought to pass and finished!

Attend now, good reader, to this story following, and note every circumstance, and thou shalt at the end perceive a wonderful work of God against such as forget Him and His benefits. Therefore, I say, consider after this my Lord Percy's troublesome business was over, and all things brought to an end. Then Mistress Anne Boleyn was again admitted to the Court, where she flourished in great estimation and favour, having always a prime grudge against my Lord Cardinal for breaking the contract between the Lord Percy and herself, supposing it had been his own device and no other's. And she at last, knowing the King's pleasure and the depth of his secrets, then began to look very haughtily, lacking no manner of rich apparel or jewels that money could purchase.

It was therefore imagined by many through the Court that she, being in such favour, might do much with the King, and obtain any suit of him for her friends. All this while, being in this estimation in all places, there was no doubt but good Queen Katherine, having this gentlewoman daily attending upon her, both heard by report and saw with her eyes how all things tended against her good Ladyship, although she seemed neither to Mistress Anne Boleyn nor the King to carry any spark of discontent or displeasure, but accepted all things in good part, and with great wisdom and much patience dissembled the same, having Mistress Anne Boleyn in more estimation for the King's sake than when she was with her before, declaring herself indeed to be a very patient Grissel, as by her long patience in all her troubles shall hereafter more plainly appear. For the King was so enamoured of this young gentlewoman that he knew not how sufficiently to advance her.

This being perceived by all the great Lords of the Court, who bore a secret grudge against my Lord Cardinal for that they could not rule in the kingdom as they would for him because he was 'Dominus factotum' with the King, and ruled as well the great Lords as the mean subjects, whereat they took occasion to work him out of the King's favour, and, consequently, themselves into more estimation. And after long and secret consultation with themselves how to bring this matter to pass, they knew very well that it was somewhat difficult for them to do absolutely of themselves. Wherefore they, perceiving the great affection and love the King bore to Mistress Anne Boleyn, supposing in their judgments that she would be a fit instrument to bring their earnest intentions to pass, therefore they often consulted with her to that purpose, and she, having both a very good wit and also an inward grudge and displeasure against my Lord Cardinal, was ever as ready to accomplish their desires as they were themselves; wherefore there was no more to do, but only to imagine an occasion to work their malice by some pretended circumstances.

Then did they daily invent divers devices how to effect their purpose, but the enterprise thereof was so dangerous, that though they would feign have attempted the matter with the King, yet durst they not, for they knew the great zeal the King did bear unto the Cardinal, and this they knew very well, that if the matter they should propound against him was not grounded upon a just and urgent cause, the King's love was such towards him, and his wit such withal, that he could with his policy vanquish all their enterprises, and then, after that, requite them in the like nature to their utter ruin.

Therefore they were compelled to forbear their plots till they might have some better ground to work upon. And now the Cardinal, seeing the great zeal the King bore to this gentlewoman, framed himself to please her as well as the King. To that end therefore he prepared great banquets and feasts to entertain the King and her at his own house, she all the while dissembling the secret grudge in her breast. Now about the Cardinal began to grow wonderful inventions, not heard of before in England, and the love between this glorious lady and the King grew to such perfection that divers things were imagined, whereof I forbear here to speak until I come to the proper place.

XI

OF THE VARIANCE BETWEEN THE FRENCH KING AND THE DUKE OF BOURBON, WHO FLED TO THE CITY OF PAVIA, WHERE THE KING BESIEGED HIM

THEN began a certain grudge between the French King and the Duke of Bourbon to break out, insomuch that the Duke, being now at variance with the house of France, was compelled for safeguard of his life to fly and forsake his country, fearing the King's malice and indignation. The Cardinal having intelligence hereof, contrived that the King our Sovereign Lord should obtain the Duke to be his General in his wars against the French King, with whom our King had then an occasion to war, and the rather because the Duke of Bourbon had fled to the Emperor to invite him to a like purpose. And after the King was advised thereof and conceived the Cardinal's invention, he mused more and more of this matter until it came into a consultation amongst the Council, so that it was concluded that an ambassador should be sent to the Emperor about this matter, and it was further concluded that the King and Emperor should join in those wars against the French King, and that the Duke of Bourbon should be the King of England's Champion and General in the field. He had a number of good soldiers over and besides the Emperor's army, which was not small, and it was agreed that the King should pay the Duke monthly wages for himself and his retinue.

For which purpose John Russell, who was afterwards created Earl of Bedford, lay continually beyond the seas in a secret place, both to receive money from the King, and to pay the same monthly to the Duke, so that the Duke began the wars with the French King in his own territories and dukedom, which the King had gotten into his own hands, being not perfectly known to the Duke's enemies that he had any aid from our Sovereign Lord; and thus he wrought the French King much displeasure, inasmuch that the French King was constrained to at once prepare an army, and in his own person to resist the Duke's power. And battle being joined, the King drove him to take Pavia, a strong town in Italy, with his host of men for his security, where the King encamped himself wonderfully strong, intending to close the Duke within the town, lest he should issue out and skirmish with him.

The French King in his camp sent secretly into England a private person (being a very witty man) to treat of a peace between his master and our Sovereign. His name was John Jokin, or Joachin, who was kept as secretly as might be, no man having intelligence of his arrival, for he was no Frenchman born, but an Italian, a man of no great estimation in France, or known to be much in his master's favour, but taken to be a merchant. And for his subtile wit he was elected to treat of such an ambassage as the French King had given him in commission.

This Jokin (or Joachin) was secretly conveyed to Richmond, and there stayed until such time as the Cardinal resorted thither to him, where, after Easter Term was ended, he kept his Feast of Whitsuntide very solemnly. In this season my Lord Cardinal caused this Jokin divers times to dine with him, who seemed to be both witty and of good behaviour; he continued long in England after this, till at last (as it should seem) he had brought the matter which he had in commission to pass, whereupon the King sent out immediately a restraint to Sir John Russell that he should retain that month's pay still in his hands, until the

King's pleasure should be further made known, which should have been paid to the Duke, being then encamped within the town of Pavia.

For want of this money the Duke and his men were much dismayed, when they saw no money come as it was wont to do; and being in this dangerous case where victuals began to be scant and very dear, they imagined many ways what should be the reason that the King's money came not. Some said this, and some said that, mistrusting nothing else than the true cause thereof.

XII

OF THE DUKE OF BOURBON'S STRATAGEM AND VICTORY, WHEREIN THE FRENCH KING WAS TAKEN PRISONER

NOW, the Duke and his soldiers were in great misery for want of victuals and other necessaries, which they could by no means get within the town. Hereupon the captains and soldiers began to grudge and murmur, being for want of victuals all like to perish; and being in this extremity, they came before the Duke and said: 'Sir, we must of force and necessity yield to our enemies; and better were it for us so to do than to starve like dogs.' But when the Duke heard this he replied with weeping tears: 'Sirs, you have proved yourselves valiant men and of noble hearts in this service, and for your necessity, whereof I myself do participate, I do not a little lament. But I shall desire you, as you are noble in heart and courage, so to take patience for two or three days, and if succour come not then from the King of England (as I doubt nothing less), I will then consent to you all to put ourselves and lives unto the mercy of our enemies.' Whereunto they all agreed, and tarried till two days were past, expecting relief from the King. Then the Duke, seeing no remedy, called his noble captains and soldiers before him, and, weeping, said: 'You noblemen and captains, we must yield ourselves unto our enemies or else famish. To yield the town and ourselves, will be to know well the cruelty of our enemies. As for my part, I care not for their cruelties, for I shall suffer death, I know very well, most cruelly if I come once into their hands. It is not, therefore, for myself that I do lament; it is for your sakes, and for your lives, and for the safeguard of your persons; for so that you might escape your enemies' hands I would willingly suffer death. Good companions and noble soldiers, I do require you all, considering the miserable calamities and dangers we are in at this present, to sell our lives most dearly rather than be murdered like beasts. Therefore, if you all consent with me, we will take upon us this night to give our enemies assault, and by that means we may either escape or else give them an overthrowal, for it were better to die like men in the field than to live prisoners miserably in captivity.' To this they all agreed.

'Then,' quoth the Duke, 'you all perceive the enemy's camp is strong, and there is no way to enter upon them but one, and that entry is planted with great cannons and strength of men so that it is impossible to attain to our enemies that way to fight with them in their camp. And also now of late you perceive they have had but small doubt of us, and so they have kept but slender watch; therefore mine advice is that there shall issue out of the town in the dead time of the night from us a certain number of you that be most likely to assault the camp, and they shall give the assault secretly against the place of the entry, which is most strong and invincible, which force and valiant assault shall be to them of the camp so doubtful that they will turn the strength of the entry that lieth over against your assault to beat you from your purpose. Then I will enter out at the postion gate and come to the place of their strength newly turned, and there ere they be aware will I enter and fight with them in the camp and win their cannon which they have newly turned, and beat them with their own pieces, and then may you come and join with me in the field.' So this device pleased them all wonderfully well, and they did then prepare themselves all that day for that device, and kept themselves secret and close without any noise or shot of pieces in the town, which gave the enemy the less fear of the assault, for at night they went all to their tents and slept quietly, nothing mistrusting what after happened. So, in the dead of the night, when they were at rest, the assailants issued out of the town, and there, according to the Duke's appointment, they gave so cruel and fierce an assault that they in the camp had much ado to withstand them. And then, as the Duke before had declared, they within were compelled to turn the shot that lay at the entry against the assault. Then issued out the Duke and with him about fifteen or sixteen hundred men or more secretly in the night, the enemy being ignorant of his coming until he entered the field. At his entry he took all the cannon that lay there and slew the gunners, then charged the pieces against the enemies, and slew them wonderfully, and cut down their tents and pavilions, and murdered many therein ere they were aware of his coming, suspecting nothing less than his entry, so that he won the field ere the King could arise. So the King was taken in his lodging before he was armed. And when the Duke had won the field, the French King being taken and his men slain, his tents robbed and spoiled and the King's coffers searched, the Duke

THE DUKE OF BOURBON'S STRATAGEM 71

of Bourbon found the league under the Great Seal of England newly made between the King of England and the French King, whereby he perceived the cause of the withdrawal of his money which should have come to him from the King, having upon due search of this matter further intelligence that all this business was devised by the Cardinal of England. Whereupon the Duke conceived such indignation against the Cardinal that he went immediately to Rome, and there intended to sack the town and to have taken the Pope; but at the first assault of the town the Duke was the first man that was there slain, notwithstanding the captains continued their assaults, and at last many of the town fled with the Pope to the Castle of Angell, where he continued in great calamity.

I have written this history more at large because that you may see whatsoever a man doth propose, be he Prince or Prelate, yet God disposeth all things according to His pleasure and will, it being a folly for any wise man to take upon him any weighty enterprise of his own will without calling upon God for His grace and assistance in all his proceedings.

I have seen Princes either when they would call a Parliament or any other great assembly that they would first call to God most reverently for His grace therein. And now I see the contrary, as it seems they trust more to their own minds and wills than to God's good grace; and even thereafter oftentimes do their matters take effect, wherefore not only in this history, but divers others, may be perceived most evident examples. Yet I see no man almost in authority or high estate regard the same, which is the greater pity and the more to be lamented. Now here I desist to speak any further of this matter, and proceed to others.

CHAPTER XIII

OF THE FRENCH KING'S REDEMPTION OUT OF CAPTIVITY, AND OF THE CARDINAL'S AMBASSAGE INTO FRANCE

UPON the taking of the French King, there were divers consultations and various opinions amongst the Council. Some held that our Sovereign Lord the King could invade the realm of France, and might easily conquer the same, forasmuch as the King with the most part of the noblemen of France were in captivity; some said, again, that the King, our Master, ought to have had the French King prisoner, forasmuch as he was taken by our King's Champion and Captain-General the Duke of Bourbon and the Emperor, insomuch that the King was advised thereby to occasion of war against the Emperor because he kept the King of France out of our King's possession, with divers imaginations and devises as their fantasies served, which were too long to relate here.

Thus were they in long consideration, whereof every man in the Court talked as his fancy served him, until at the last divers ambassadors from the realm of France came to the King, our Lord, desiring him to take order with the Emperor for the French King's delivery as his Highness's wisdom should think best, wherein my Lord Cardinal bore great rule. So that after great deliberation and advice being taken, it was thought good by the Cardinal that the Emperor should deliver the French King out of his ward upon sufficient pledges.

And afterwards it was thought meet that the King's two sons, that is to say the Dauphin and the Duke of Orleans, should be delivered as hostages for security of the Emperor and the King our Sovereign Lord upon all such demands and requests as should be demanded of the French King as well by the Emperor as by our Sovereign Lord.

The Cardinal, lamenting the French King's captivity and the Pope's great adversity (who yet remained in the Castle Angell, either as prisoner or else for defence against his enemies), endeavoured and laboured all that he could with the King and his Council to take some order for the benefit of them both.

At the last, as you have heard before, divers of the great States and Lords of the Council, with the Lady Anne, lay in continual wait to spy a convenient occasion to take the Cardinal in a snare.

Therefore they consulted with the Cardinal, and informed him that they thought it a necessary time for him to take upon him the King's commission to travel beyond the seas, and by his wisdom to compass a present peace amongst these great princes and potentates, encouraging him thereto and alleging that it was more meet for his wisdom, discretion and authority to bring so weighty a matter to pass than for any other within the realm. Their intent was no other than to get him from the King that they might adventure, by the help of their chief mistresses, to malign him unto the King, and so in his absence bring him into his disgrace, or at the least to be in less estimation.

Well, the matter was so handled that the Cardinal was commanded to prepare himself for the journey which he took upon him, but whether willingly or not I cannot say. But this I know, that he made so short abode after the perfect resolution thereof that he caused all things to be prepared speedily for his journey; and every one of his servants was appointed that should attend him in the same.

When all things were concluded and provided

for this noble journey, he advanced forward in the name of God; my Lord had with him such of the Lords and Bishops as were not of the conspiracy.

Then marched he forward from his new house at Westminster through all London, over London Bridge, having a great many of gentlemen in a rank before him in velvet coats, and the most part of them with chains of gold about their necks. And all his yeomen followed him with noble men and tall men-servants, all in orange-tawny coats, and the Cardinal's hat with T. and C. for Thomas Cardinal embroidered upon them and also upon his own servants' coats, and those of the rest of the gentlemen. His sumpter mules were twenty and more in number, and when all his carriages and carts and other train were passed before, he rode very sumptuously, like a Cardinal, with the rest of his train, on his mule, with his spare mule and his spare horse covered with crimson velvet and gilt stirrups following him. And before him he had his two great silver crosses, his two pillars of silver, the King's Broad Seal of England and his Cardinal's hat, and a gentleman carrying his valaunce, otherwise called his cloak-bag, which was made of fine scarlet all embroidered very richly with gold. Thus he passed through London, as I said before, and all the way in his journey he was thus furnished, having his harbingers in every place before, which prepared lodgings for him and his said train.

The first journey he went two miles beyond Deptford in Kent, unto Sir Richard Wiltshire's house; the rest of his train were lodged in Deptford, and in the country thereabouts.

The next day he marched to Rochester, where he lay in the Bishop's Palace, and the rest were lodged in the city.

The third day he rode from thence to Faversham, and there lodged in the Abbey, and his train in the town, and some about in the country.

The fourth day he rode to Canterbury, where he was kindly entertained by the Bishop of the city, and there he continued four or five days; in which season was the Jubilee and a great fair in the town, by reason it was the Feast of Saint Thomas, their patron, upon which day there was a solemn procession, wherein my Lord Cardinal was in his Legatine ornaments, with his hat upon his head, who commanded the monks and the choir to sing the Latin after this sort: 'Sancta Maria ora pro Papa nostro clemente'; and in this manner perused the Latin through, my Lord Cardinal kneeling at a stool before the choir door prepared for him with carpets and cushions. All the monks and the choir stood in the body singing the Litany; at which time I saw my Lord Cardinal weep tenderly, the which many conceived to be for grief that the Pope was in such calamity and danger of the Lance Knights. The next day I was sent with letters from my Lord to a Cardinal in Calais in post, so that I was the same night in Calais. At my arrival I found standing upon the pier without the Lantern Gate all the Council of the town, to whom I delivered up my message and my letters before I entered the town, where I lay until my Lord came thither, who arrived two days after my coming thither before eight o'clock in the morning, and was received of all the noble Officers and Council of the town with procession, the clerks being in rich copes having many rich crosses. In the Lantern Gate a stool with cushions and carpets was set for him, where he kneeled and made his prayers, at which time they censed him with censers of silver and sprinkled water. That done, they passed on before him in procession until he came into Saint Mary's Church, where, at the High Altar, turning him to the people, he gave them his Benediction and pardon, and then he repaired with a great number of noblemen and gentlemen to a place in the town called the Chequer, where he kept his house so long as he abode in the town, going immediately into his bed, because he was somewhat troubled with sickness by reason of his passage by sea.

That night he called unto him Monsieur de Biez, Captain of Boulogne, with divers other gallants and gentlemen who had dined with him that day, and having some further consultation with my Lord Cardinal, he and the rest of the gentlemen departed again to Boulogne.

Thus my Lord was daily visited with one or other of the French nobility.

When all his train and carriage was landed, and all things prepared for his journey, His Grace called all his noblemen and gentlemen into the Privy Chamber, where, being assembled before him, he said: 'I have called you hither to declare unto you that I would have you both consider the duty you owe to me and the goodwill I openly bear to you for the same. I would show you further the authority I have by commission from the King, your diligent observance of which I will hereafter recommend to His Majesty, as also to show you the nature of the Frenchmen, and withal to instruct you what reverence you shall show me for the high honour of the King's majesty, and to inform you how you shall entertain and accompany the Frenchmen when you meet at any time.

'Concerning the first point, you shall understand for divers weighty affairs of His Grace's, and for mere advancement of his royal dignity, he hath assigned me in this journey to be his Lieutenant.

What reverence belongeth to me for the same I will show you.

'By virtue therefore of my commission and Lieutenantship, I assume and take upon me to be esteemed in all honour and degrees of service as unto His Highness is meet and due, and that by me nothing be neglected that to his State is due and fitting; for my part you shall see that I will not omit one jot thereof. Therefore, one of the chief causes of your assembly at this time is to inform you that you be not ignorant of your duty in this. I wish you, therefore, as you would have my favour, and also charge you all in the King's name, that you do not forget the same in time and place, but that every one of you do observe his duty to me according as you will at your return avoid the King's indignation or deserve His Highness's thanks, the which I will set forth at our return as each of you shall deserve.

'Now, to the second point, the nature of Frenchmen is such that at their first meeting they will be as familiar with you as if they had known you by long acquaintance, and will commune with you in their French tongue as if you knew every word; therefore use them in a kind manner, and be as familiar with them as they are with you. If they speak to you in their natural tongue, speak to them in English; for if you understand not them, no more shall they you.' Then, speaking merrily to one of the gentlemen, being a Welshman, 'Rice,' quoth he, 'speak thou Welsh to them, and doubt not but thy speech will be more difficult to them than their French shall be to thee.' Moreover, he said unto them all, 'Let your entertainment and behaviour be according to all gentlemen's in humility that it may be reported after our departure from thence that you were gentlemen of very good behaviour and humility, that all men may know you understand your duties to your King and to your master; thus shall you not only obtain to yourselves great commendations and praises, but also greatly advance your Prince and country.

'Now, being admonished of these things, prepare yourselves against to-morrow, for then we purpose to set forward.' Therefore we his servants, being thus instructed and all things being in readiness, proceeded forwards.

The next day being Mary Magdalen's Day, my Lord Cardinal advanced out of Calais with such a number of black coats as hath seldom been seen; with the ambassador went all the Peers of Calais and Guienne. All other gentlemen, besides those of his train, were garnished with black velvet coats and chains of gold.

Thus passed he forward, with his troop before,

three in a rank, which compass extended three quarters of a mile in length, having his crosses and all of his other accustomed glorious furniture carried before him, as I have formerly related, except the Broad Seal, the which he left with Doctor Taylor, then Master of the Rolls, until his return.

Thus passing on his way, we had scarce gone a mile but it began to rain so vehemently that I have not seen the like for the time, which endured until we came to Boulogne, and ere we came to Standingfield the Cardinal of Lorraine, a goodly young gentleman, gave my Lord a meeting and received him with much joy and reverence, and so passed forth with my Lord in communication, until we came near the said Standingfield, which is a religious place standing between the English, French and imperial dominions, being a neuter, held of neither of them.

Then there we waited for my Lord the Count Brion, Captain of Picardy, with a great number of Stradiots or Arbenois,* standing in array in a great field of green oats, all in harness upon light horses, passing on with my Lord in a wing unto Boulogne and so after into Picardy, for my Lord doubted that the Emperor would lay some ambush to

* Stradiots and Arbenois were light-armed cavalry, said to be Greek mercenaries.

betray him, for which cause he commanded them to attend my Lord for the safety of his own person, to conduct him from the danger of his enemies.

Thus rode he accompanied until he came nigh to Boulogne, within an English mile, where all the worshipful citizens of Boulogne came and met him, having a learned man that made an oration in Latin to him, unto the which my Lord made answer; and that done, Monsieur de Biez, Captain of Boulogne, with his retinue, met him on horseback with all his assembly. Thus he marched into the town, alighting at the Abbey gate, from whence he was conveyed into the Abbey with procession, and they presented him with the image of Our Lady, commonly called Our Lady of Boulogne, where were always great offerings. That done, he gave his blessing to the people with certain days of pardon. Then went he into the Abbey to his lodging, but all his train were lodged in the high and basse towns.

The next day, after he had heard Mass, he rode to Montreuil, where he was in like manner saluted by the worshipful of the town all in livery alike, where also a learned oration was made to him in Latin, which His Grace answered, again in Latin. And as he entered in at the gate there was a canopy of silk embroidered with like letters as his men had on their coats. And when he was alighted, his footmen had it as due to their office. There was also made pageants for joy of his coming, who was called in the French tongue whither ever he rode or came 'Le Cardinal de Patifagus,' and in Latin 'Cardinalis Patifagus,' who was accompanied all that night with the gentlemen of the country thereabout.

The next day he took his journey towards Abbeville, where he was in like manner entertained and conveyed into the town, and most honourably welcomed with divers kinds of pageants both costly and wittily contrived at every turning of the streets, as he rode through the town, having a canopy borne over him richer than at Montreuil; and so they conveyed him to his lodging, which was a fair house newly built with brick, at which house the French King Louis was married to the King's sister, who was married after to the Duke of Suffolk. In this town of Abbeville he remained eight or nine days, where resorted unto him divers of the French King's Council, every day continually feasting and entertaining him and the other Lords. At the time of his departing out of the town, he rode to a castle beyond the water, called by some the Channel Percequeine, standing and adjoining to the said water upon a great hill and rock, within the which there was a college of priests, the situation whereof was much like to the Castle of

Windsor in England, and there he was received with a solemn procession, conveying him first to the church and then to the castle upon the bridge over the water of Somme, where Edward IV. met with the French King, as you may read at large in the Chronicles of England.

My Lord was no sooner seated in his lodging, but I heard that the French King would come that day to the city of Amiens, which was not above six English miles from thence. And being desirous to see his coming thither, I took with me two of my Lord's gentlemen, and rode presently thither. Being but strangers, we took up our lodgings at the sign of the Angel, directly over against the west door of the cathedral church of Nôtre Dame, where we stayed in expectation of the King's coming. And about four of the clock came Madam Regent, the King's mother, riding in a very rich chariot, and with her within was the Queen of Navarre, her daughter, attended with a hundred or more of ladies and gentlewomen, following, every one riding upon a white palfrey; also her guard, which was of no small number.

And within two days after the King came in with a shot of guns, and there were divers pageants made only for joy of his coming, having about his person and before him a great number of noblemen and gentlemen in three companies. The first were of Soutches and Burgonians with guns, the second were Frenchmen with bows, the third guard was of tall Scots, who were more comely persons than all the rest. The French guard and Scottish had all one livery, being apparelled with rich coats of white cloth, with a rich guard of silver bullion of a handful broad. The King came riding on a rich genet, and did alight at the said great church, and was conveyed with procession to the Bishop's palace, where he was lodged.

The next morning I rode again to Pincquigny to attend upon my Lord, and when I came, my Lord was ready to go on horseback to ride towards Amiens, and, passing on his way, was saluted by divers noble personages, making him orations in Latin, to whom my Lord made answer 'extempore.' There was word brought him that the King was ready to meet him, wherefore he had no other shift but to alight at an old chapel that stood hard by the highway, and there he newly apparelled himself in rich array, and so mounted again upon another mule, very richly trapped with a foot-cloth of crimson velvet purled with gold, and fringed about the edges with a fringe of gold very costly; his stirrups of silver gilt; the bosses of the same and the checks of his mule's bit were all gilt with fine gold, and by the time he was mounted again in this gorgeous manner the King was come very near, within less than an English quarter of a mile, his guard standing in array upon the top of a high hill, expecting my Lord's coming, to whom my Lord made as much haste as conveniently he could, until he came within a pair of butt lengths, and there he stayed. The King perceiving that, caused Monsieur Vaudemont to issue from him and to ride to my Lord Cardinal to know the cause of his tarrying; and so Monsieur Vaudemont, being mounted upon a very fair genet, took his race with his horse till he came even to my Lord, and then he caused his horse to come aloft twice or thrice so near my Lord's mule that he was in doubt of his horse, and so alighted, and in humble reverence did his message to my Lord. That done, he repaired to the King. And then the King advanced forwards, seeing my Lord do the like, and in the mid-way they met, embracing each other with amiable countenances. Then came into the place all noblemen and gentlemen on both sides, who made a mighty press.

Then the King's officers cried:

'Marche, marche, devant, allez devant!'

So the King, with the Lord Cardinal on his right hand, rode towards Amiens, every English gentleman being accompanied by another of France. The train of these two great princes was two miles in length—that is to say, from the place of their meeting at Amiens, where they were nobly received with guns and pageants, until the King had brought my Lord to his lodging, and then departed for the night, the King being lodged in the Bishop's Palace. And the next day, after dinner, my Lord rode with a great train of English noblemen and gentlemen unto the Court to the King, at which time the King kept his bed, yet nevertheless my Lord came into his bedchamber, where on the one side of the bed sat the King's mother, and on the other side the Cardinal of Lorraine, accompanied with divers other gentlemen of France, and after some communication and drinking of wine with the King's mother, my Lord departed and returned to his own lodging, accompanied with divers other lords and gentlemen.

Thus continued my Lord at Amiens, and also the King, fourteen days, feasting each other divers times, and there one day at Mass the King and my Lord received the Holy Sacrament, as also the Queen Regent and the Queen of Navarre. After that it was determined that the King and my Lord should remove, and so they rode to a city called Compeigne, which was more than twenty miles from Amiens, unto which town I was sent to provide lodging for my Lord, and in my travel I had occasion to stay by the way at a little village to shoe my horse. There came to me a servant from the Castle, perceiving me to be an Englishman and one of my Lord Legate's servants, who desired me to go into the Castle to the Lord, his master, whom he thought would be very glad to see me, to whom I consented because I desired acquaintance with strangers, especially men of authority and honourable rank; so I went with him, who conducted me to the Castle, and at my first entrance I was among the watchmen who kept the first ward, being very tall men and comely persons, who saluted me very kindly.

Knowing the cause of my coming, they advertised their lord and master, and forthwith the lord of the castle came out unto me. His name was Monsieur Crookesly, a nobleman born, and at his coming he embraced me, saying that I was heartily welcome, and thanked me that I was so gentle as to visit him and his castle, saying that he was preparing to meet the King and my Lord Cardinal, and to invite them to his castle; and when he had showed me the strength of his castle and the walls, which were fourteen feet broad, and I had seen all the houses, he brought me down into a fair inner court, where his genet stood ready for him, with twelve other of the fairest genets that ever I saw, especially his own, which was a mare, for which genet he told me he had 400 crowns offered. Upon these twelve genets were mounted twelve goodly gentlemen, called pages of honour. They rode all bareheaded in coats of cloth of gold, guarded with black velvet, and they had all of them boots of red Spanish leather.

Then took he his leave of me, commanding his Steward and other of his gentlemen to conduct me to his lady to dinner. So they led me up to the gatehouse, where then their lady and mistress lay for the time that the King and the Cardinal should tarry there. And after a short time the Lady Crookesly came out of her chamber into the dining-room, where I attended her coming, who did receive me very nobly, she having a train of twelve gentlemen that did attend on her.

'Forasmuch,' quoth she, 'as you are an Englishman, whose custom is to kiss all the ladies and gentlewomen in your country without offence, yet it is not so in this realm; notwithstanding, I will be so bold as to kiss you, and so shall you salute all my maids.'

After this we went to dinner, being nobly served as ever I saw in England, passing all dinner-time in pleasing discourses.

And shortly after dinner I took my leave, and was constrained that night to lie short of Compeigne at a great walled town called Montdidier, the suburbs whereof my Lord of Suffolk had lately burned, and early in the morning I came to Compeigne, being Saturday and market-day. At my first coming I took up my inn over against the market-place, and being set at dinner in a fair chamber that looked out into the street, I heard a great noise and clattering of bills, and looking out, I saw the officers of the town bringing a prisoner to execution, and with a sword cut off his head. I demanded what was the offence. They answered me, for killing of red-deer in the forest near adjoining. And immediately they held the poor man's head upon a pole in the market-place between the stag's horns, and his four quarters were set up in four places of the forest.

Having prepared my Cardinal's lodgings in the great castle of the town, and seen it furnished, my Lord had the one half assigned, and the King the other half, and in like manner they divided the gallery between them. And in the midst thereof there was made a strong wall, with a window and a door, where the King and my Lord did often meet and talk, and divers times go one to the other through the same door. Also there was lodged in the same castle Madam Regent, the King's mother, and all the ladies and gentlewomen that did attend on her.

Not long after came the Lord Chancellor of France, a very witty man, with all the King's grave Counsellors, and they took great pains daily in consultation. At which time I heard my Lord Cardinal fall out with the Chancellor of France, laying to his charge that he went about to hinder the League which before his coming was concluded upon by the King, our Sovereign Lord, and the French King, their master, insomuch that my Lord told him it was not he that should infringe the amiable friendship; and if the French King, his master, being there present, would follow his, the Chancellor's, counsel, he should not fail shortly after his return to feel the smart which it was to maintain war against the King of England, and thereof he should be well assured. He arose and went unto his own lodging wondrously offended insomuch that his angry speech and bold countenance made them all doubt how to quiet him to the Council, who was then departed in great fury. Now here was sending, here was coming, here was entreating, and here was great submission and intercession made unto him to reduce him to his former communication, who would in no ways relent until Madam Regent came to him herself, who handled the matter so well that she brought him to his former communication, and by this means he brought all things to pass that before he could not compass, which was more out of fear than affection the French King had to the matter in hand, for now he had got the heads of the Council under his girdle.

The next morning after this conflict the Cardinal arose about four of the clock and sate him down to write letters into England unto the King, commanding one of his Chaplains to prepare himself ready, insomuch that the Chaplain stood ready in his vestments until four of the clock in the afternoon, all which season my Lord never rose to any meat, but continually wrote letters with his own hand. About four o'clock of the afternoon he made an end of writing, commanding one Christopher Gunner, the King's Sergeant, to prepare himself without delay to ride post into England with his letters, whom he despatched away ere ever he drank. That done, he went to Mass and Matins and other devotions with his Chaplain, as he was accustomed to do, and then went to walk in a garden the space of an hour or more, and then said Evening Song, and so went to dinner and supper, making no long stay, and so went to bed.

The next night following my Lord caused a great supper to be made, or rather a banquet, for Madam Regent and the Queen of Navarre and other noble personages, lords and ladies; at which supper was Madam Louis, one of the daughters of Louis, the last King, whose sister lately died. These two sisters were by their mother inheritors of the Duchy of Brittany. And forasmuch as King Francis had married one of the sisters, by which he had one moiety of the said Duchy, he kept the said Madam Louis, the other sister, without marriage, to the intent that the whole Duchy might descend to him or his successors after his death for lack of issue of her.

But now let us return to the supper or banquet where all those noble personages were highly feasted. And in the midst of the said banquet the French King and the King of Navarre came suddenly in, who took their places in the lowest part thereof. There was not only plenty of fine meats, but also much mirth and solace as well in merry communication as also the noise of my Lord's music, who played there all that night so cunningly that the two Kings took great delight therein, insomuch that the French King desired my Lord to lend them unto him for the next night. And after the supper or banquet was ended the lords fell to dancing, amongst whom one Madam Fontaine had the praise. And thus passed they the most part of the night ere they parted.

The next day the King took my Lord's music and rode to a nobleman's house, where was some goodly image to whom he had vowed a night's pilgrimage. And to perform his devotion when he came there (which was in the night) he danced and caused others to do the same, and the next morning he returned to Compeigne.

The King, being at Compeigne, gave order that a wild boar should be lodged for him in the forest, whither my Lord Cardinal went with him to see him hunt the wild boar, where the Lady Regent, with a number of ladies and damsels, were standing, in chariots, looking upon the toil. Amongst these ladies stood my Lord Cardinal to regard the hunting in the Lady Regent's chariot, and within the toil was the King, with divers ladies of France ready furnished for the high and perilous enterprise of hunting this dangerous wild swine.

The King was in his doublet and hose, all of sheep's-colour cloth, richly trimmed, in his slip a brace of very great greyhounds, who were armed as their manner is to defend them from the violence of the beasts' tusks. And the rest of the King's gentlemen that were appointed to hunt were likewise in their doublets and hose, holding each of them a very sharp boar's spear. Then the King commanded the keepers to set free the boar, and that every person within the toil should go to a standing, amongst whom were divers gentlemen of England.

The boar presently issued out of his den, and, being pursued by a hound, came into the plain, where he stayed awhile, gazing upon the people, and the hound, drawing near him, he espied a bush upon a bank. Under the bush lay two Frenchmen, who fled thither, thinking there to be safe; but the boar, smelling them, thrust his head into the bush, and these two men came away from thence as men are accustomed to fly from the danger of death.

Then was the boar, by the violence of the hunters, driven from thence, who ran straight to one of my Lord's footmen, a very tall man, who had in his hand an English javelin, with which he defended himself a great while. But the boar continued foaming at him with his great tusks; at the last the boar broke in sunder his javelin, so that he was glad to draw his sword and therewith stood upon his guard, until the hunters came and rescued him and put the boar once again to flight, to another gentleman of England, one Mr. Ratcliffe, who was son and heir to the Lord Fitzwalter, now Earl of Sussex, who by his boar's spear rescued himself. There were many other passages, but I forbear prolixity, and return to the matter in hand.

Many days were spent in consultation and expectation of Christopher Gunner's return, who was formerly sent post into England with letters, as I said before. At last he returned with letters, upon receipt whereof my Lord prepared with all expedition to return to England. The morning that my Lord intended to remove, being at Mass in his closet, he consecrated the Chancellor of France a Cardinal, and put his hat on his head and his cap of scarlet, and then took his journey, and returned into England with all expedition he could, and came to Guienne, and was there nobly entertained of my Lord Sands, who was Captain of that place, and from thence went to Calais, where he stayed awhile for shipping of his goods. And in the meantime he established a mart to be there kept for all nations. But how long, or in what sort it continued, I know not, for I never heard of any good it did or of any assembly of merchants or traffic of merchandise that were brought thither, for so great and mighty a matter as was intended for the good of the town. This being established, he took shipping for Dover, and from thence rode post to Court.

The King was then in his progress at Sir Henry Wyatt's house, in Kent, of whom I and other of his servants thought the Cardinal should have been nobly entertained as well of the King as of his nobles. But we were all deceived in our expectations. Notwithstanding, he went immediately to the King after his return, with whom he had long talk, and continued two or three days after in the Court, and then retired to his house at Westminster, where he remained till Michaelmas term, which was within a fortnight after, and there he exercised his place of Chancellorship, as he had done before.

And immediately after the beginning of the term he caused to be assembled in the Starchamber all the noblemen, judges, and justices of the peace of every shire throughout England, and were at Westminster Hall then present. And there he made a long oration, declaring the cause of his ambassage into France, and of his proceedings therein, saying that he had concluded such an amity and peace as never was heard of in this realm between our Sovereign Lord the King's Majesty, the Emperor, and the French King, for a perpetual peace which shall be confirmed in writing, under the Seals of both realms engraven in gold, and offered further that our King should receive yearly by that same out of the Duchy of Normandy all the charges and losses he had sustained in the wars.

And also forasmuch as there was a restraint made of the French Queen's dowry (whom the Duke of Suffolk had married) for many years together during the wars, it was concluded that she should not only receive the same according to her just right, but all the arrears being unpaid during the said restraint should be perfected shortly after. The resort of Ambassadors out of France should be such a great number of noblemen and gentlemen to confirm the same as hath not been seen heretofore to repair thither out of one realm.

This peace concluded, there shall be such an amity between them of each realm and intercourse of merchandise that it shall be seen to all men to be but one monarchy. Gentlemen and others may travel from one country to another for their recreations and pleasure. Merchants also of either country may traffic safely without fear of danger, so that this realm shall ever after flourish. Therefore may all Englishmen well rejoice and set forth the truth of this embassy in the country.

'Now, my masters, I beseech you and require you in the King's behalf that you show yourselves as loving and obedient subjects in whom the King may much rejoice.'

And so he ended his oration and broke up the Court for that time.

XIV

OF THE FRENCH AMBASSADOR'S ENTERTAINMENT AND DESPATCH

NOW the great long-looked-for ambassadors are arrived, being in number eight persons of the noblest and most worthy gentlemen in all France, who were nobly received from place to place, and so conveyed through London to the Bishop's palace in St. Paul's Churchyard, where they were lodged, to whom divers noblemen resorted and gave them noble presents (especially the Mayor of London), as wines, sugars, beef, mutton, capons, wild fowl, wax and other necessary things in abundance for the expenses of his house. They resorted to the Court, being then at Greenwich, on Sunday, and were received of the King's Majesty, of whom they were entertained highly.

They had a commission to establish our King's Highness in the order of France, to whom they brought for that intent a collar of fine gold with a Michael hanging thereat, and robes to the said order appertaining, which were of blue velvet and richly embroidered, wherein I saw the King pass to the closet and after in the same to Mass.

And to gratify the French King for his great honour, he sent at once noble men here in England of the Order of the Garter, which Garter the Herald carried into France unto the French King, to establish him in the Order of the Garter and robes according to the same, the French Ambassador still remaining here until the return of the English. All these things being then determined and concluded concerning the perpetual peace upon solemn ceremonies and oaths contained in certain documents concerning the same, it was concluded that there should be solemn Mass sung in the Cathedral Church of St. Paul's in London by the Cardinal, the King being present at the same in his travers to perform all things determined.

And for the preparation thereof, there was a gallery from the west door of St. Paul's Church through the body of the same up to the choir and to the High Altar into the transepts.

My Lord Cardinal prepared himself to sing the Mass, associated with twenty-four mitred Bishops and Abbots, who attended him with such ceremonies as to him were then due by reason of his Legatine prerogative.

And after the last Agnus the King rose out of the travers and kneeled upon a carpet and cushions before the High Altar, and the like did the great Master of France, chief Ambassador, that here represented the King's person of France. Between them the Lord Cardinal divided the Blessed Sacrament as a perfect oath and bond for security of the said Covenants of perpetual peace. That done, the King went again into the travers. This Mass being ended, which was solemnly sung by the choir of the same church and all the King's chapel, then my Lord took and read the Articles of Peace openly before the King and all others, both English and French, and there in sight of all the people the King put his hand to the Gold Seal and subscribed with his own hand and delivered the same to the Grand Master of France, as his deed, who openly did the like. That done, they departed and rode home with the Cardinal and dined with him, passing all the day after in consultation of weighty affairs touching the Articles and conclusion of the said peace.

Then the King departed to Greenwich by water, at whose departure it was concluded by the King's device that all the Frenchmen should remove to Richmond and hunt there, and from thence to

Hampton Court, and there to hunt likewise. And the Lord Cardinal was there to make a banquet or supper or both, and from thence they should ride to Windsor and there hunt, and after return to the King at Greenwich, and there to banquet with him before their departure.

This determined, they all repaired to their lodgings; then was there no more to do but to make preparation in all things for the entertainment of this great assembly at Hampton Court, at the time appointed by my Lord Cardinal, who called before him all his chief officers, as stewards, treasurers, clerks and comptrollers of his kitchen, to whom he declared his whole mind touching the entertainment of the Frenchmen at Hampton Court, to whom he also gave command neither to spare for any cost or expenses or pains to make them such a triumphant banquet, as they might not only wonder at it here, but also make a glorious report to the great honour of our King and this realm.

Thus having made known his pleasure, to accomplish his commandment, they sent out all the carriers, purveyors and other persons to my Lord's friends to prepare; also they sent to all expert cooks and cunning persons in the arts of cookery in London or elsewhere, that they might be secured to beautify the noble feast.

Then the purveyor provided and my Lord's friends sent in such provision that it was a wonder to see it. The cooks wrought both day and night in many curious devices, and there was no lack of gold, silver or any other costly thing; the yeomen and grooms of his wardrobe were busied in hanging the chambers with costly hangings, and furnished the same with beds of silk and other furniture for the same of every kind.

Then my Lord sent me, being his Gentleman Usher, and two other of my fellows to foresee all things touching our rooms to be richly garnished, wherein our pains were not small, but daily we travelled up and down from chamber to chamber to see things fitted.

Then wrought joiners, carpenters, painters, and other artificers needful, so that there was nothing wanting to adorn this noble feast. There was carriage and re-carriage of plate, stuff, and other rich ornaments, so that there was nothing lacking that could be devised or imagined for the purpose.

There were also provided two hundred and eighty beds, with all manner of furniture, too long here to be related. The day assigned to the Frenchmen being come, they were ready assembled before the hour of their appointment, wherefore the officers caused them to ride to Hanworth, a park of the King's within three miles of Hampton Court, there to spend the time in hunting till night, which they did, and then returned, and every one of them were conveyed to their several chambers, having in them good fires and store of wine, where they remained till supper was ready.

The chambers where they supped and banqueted were adorned thus. First, the great waiting-chamber was hung with very rich cloth of Arras, and so all the rest, some better than others, and they were furnished with tall yeomen to serve. There were set tables around the chambers, banquet-wise covered; also a cupboard garnished with white plates; also in the same chamber were four great plates, to give the more light, set with great lights, a great fire of wood and coals.

The next chamber was the Chamber of Presence, richly hung also with cloth of Arras, and a sumptuous cloth of state, furnished with many goodly gentlemen to serve. The tables were ordered in manner as the other were, save only the high table was removed beneath the cloth of state, towards the midst of the chamber, with six desks of plate, garnished all over with fine gold, having one pair of candlesticks of silver and gilt with lights in the same; the cupboard was barred about so that no man could come very near it, for there were divers pieces of plate of great store to use besides. The plates that hung on the walls to give light were silver and gilt with wax lights.

Now were all things in readiness, and the supper being set, the principal officers caused the trumpets to blow to call them to supper. The officers conducted the noblemen to where they were to sup, and they being set, service came up in such abundance, both costly and full of devices, with such a pleasant noise of music that the Frenchmen (as it seemed) were rapt up in a heavenly paradise. You must understand that my Lord Cardinal was not there all this while. But the French messieurs were very merry with their rich fare. But before the second course, my Lord Cardinal came in booted and spurred suddenly amongst them, at whose coming there was great joy, every man rising from his place, whom my Lord Cardinal caused to sit still and keep their places. Being in his riding apparel, he called for his chair and sat him down in the midst of the high table, and was there as merry and pleasant as ever I saw him in my life.

Presently after came up the second course, which was above one hundred different devices, which were so goodly and costly that I think the Frenchmen never saw the like. But the rarest curiosities of all the rest (which, indeed, was worthy of wonder) were castles with images in the same like St. Paul's Church; there were also beasts, birds, fowls, personages, most excellently made, some fighting with swords, some with guns, others with cross-bows, some dancing with ladies, some on horseback with complete armour, jousting with long and sharp spears, and many other strange devices, which I cannot describe. Amongst all I noted there was a chess-board subtilely made of spiced plate with men to the same. And because Frenchmen are very expert at that sport, my Lord Cardinal gave that same to a French gentleman, commanding that there should be made a good care to convey the same into his country.

Then called my Lord for a great bowl of gold filled with Hippocras, and putting off his cap, said: 'I drink a health to the King my Sovereign Lord, and next unto the King your Master.' And when he had drunk a hearty draught, he desired the Grand Master to pledge him a cup, which cup was worth five hundred marks, and so all the Lords in order pledged these great princes.

Then went the cup merrily about, so that many of these Frenchmen were led to their beds; then went my Lord to his Privy Chamber, making a short supper, or rather a short repast, and then returned again into the Presence Chamber amongst the Frenchmen, behaving himself in such a loving sort and so familiarly towards them, that they could not sufficiently commend him.

And while they were in communication and pastime, all their livery were served to their chambers; each chamber had a basin and ewer of silver and a great silver pot with plenty of wine and sufficient of everything.

Thus furnished was every room about the house; when all was done, then were they conducted to their lodgings. In the morning after they had heard Mass, they stayed and dined with my Lord, and so departed towards Windsor. And as soon as they were gone, my Lord returned to London, because it was the midst of the term.

You must conceive the King was privy to this magnificent feast, who then intended far to exceed the same, which I leave till the Frenchmen's return. Now, the King had given command to his officers to provide a far more sumptuous banquet for the strangers than they had at the Cardinal's, which was not neglected. After the return of these strangers from Windsor—which place they much commended for the situation thereof—the King invited them to the Court, where they dined, and after dinner they danced and had their pastime till supper-time.

Then was the banquet-chamber in the little yard at Greenwich furnished for the entertainment of these strangers, to which place they were conducted by the greatest personages then being in the Court, where they did both sup and banquet, but to describe to you the order hereof, the variety of costly dishes, and the curious devices, my weak ability and shallow capacity would much eclipse the magnificence thereof. But thus much take notice of, that although that banquet at Hampton Court was marvellously sumptuous, yet this banquet excelled the same as much as gold doth silver in value. And for my part I never saw the like.

In the midst of the banquet there was turning at the barriers of lusty gentlemen, very gorgeous on foot, and the like on horseback. And after all this there was such an excellent interlude made in Latin that I never saw or heard the like, the actors' apparel being so gorgeous and of such strange devices that it passeth my poor capacity to relate them.

This being ended, there came a great company of ladies and gentlewomen, the chiefest beauties in the realm of England, being as richly attired as cost could make or art devise to set forth their gestures, proportions, or beauty, that they seemed to the beholder rather like celestial angels than terrestrial creatures, and, in my judgment, worthy of admiration, with whom the gentlemen of France danced and masked, every man choosing as his fancy served. That done, and the maskers departed, there came in another mask of ladies and gentlewomen more richly attired than I can express. These lady maskers took each of them one of the Frenchmen to dance with; and here note that these noble women spoke all of them good French, and it delighted the Frenchmen much to hear the ladies speak to them in their own language. Thus triumphantly did they spend the whole night from five of the clock at night unto two or three of the clock in the morning, at which time the gallants drew all to their lodgings to take their rest.

As neither health, wealth, nor pleasure can always last, so ended this triumphant banquet, which, being past, seemed in the morning to the beholders as a fantastic dream.

Now, after all this solemn banqueting, they prepared with bag and baggage to return, and thereupon repaired to the King, and, in order, every man took his leave of His Majesty and the nobles, by whom the King sent his princely pleasure and commendations to the King their Master, thanked them for their pains, and after great communications with the Great Master of that Ambassage, he bade them adieu. Then they came to Westminster to my Lord Cardinal to do the like, of whom he received the King's reward, which I shall hereafter relate.

First every man of honour and estimation had plate, some to the value of two or three hundred pounds, and some of four hundred pounds, besides the great gifts before received of His Majesty, such as gowns of velvet with rich furs, great chains of gold; and some had goodly horses of great value, with divers other gifts of great value which I cannot call to remembrance, but the least of them had the sum of twenty crowns, and thus being nobly rewarded, my Lord, after humble commendation of them to the French King, bade them farewell; and so they departed. The next day they were conveyed to Dover to the seaside, with all their furniture, being accompanied with many English young gallants, and what report of their royal entertainment they made in their own country I never heard.

XV

OF THE KING'S DISCOVERY OF HIS LOVE FOR MISTRESS ANNE BOLEYN TO THE CARDINAL, WITH THE CARDINAL'S DISLIKE, AND ALSO THE OPINION OF ALL LEARNED BISHOPS IN ENGLAND AND FOREIGN UNIVERSITIES

AFTER this began new matters which troubled the heads and imaginations of all the Court—namely, the long-concealed affection of the King for Mistress Anne Boleyn now broke out, which His Majesty disclosed to the Cardinal, whose frequent persuasions on his knees took no effect. My Lord thereupon being compelled to declare to His Majesty his opinion and wisdom in the advancement of the King's desires, thought it not safe for him to wade too far alone, or to give rash judgment in so weighty a matter, but desired leave of the King to ask counsel of men of ancient and famous learning both in divine and civil laws.

Now, this being obtained, he by his Legatine authority sent out his commissions for the Bishops of this realm, who not long after assembled all at Westminster before my Lord Cardinal. And not only these Prelates, but also the most learned men of both Universities, and some from divers cathedral colleges in this realm who were thought sufficiently able to solve this doubtful question. At this learned assembly was the King's case consulted of, debated, argued, and judged from day to day. But in conclusion, when these ancient Fathers of Law and Divinity parted, they were all of one judgment, and that contrary to the expectation of most men. And I heard some of the most famous and learned amongst them say the King's case was too obscure for any man, and the points therein were doubtful to have any resolution therein, and so at that time with a general consent departed without any resolution or judgment. In this assembly of Bishops and divers learned men it was thought very expedient that the King should send out his Commissioners into all Universities in Christendom, as well here in England as in foreign regions, there to have this case argued substantially, and to bring with them from thence every definition of their opinions of the same under the Seal of every University.

And thereupon divers Commissioners were immediately despatched for this purpose. Some were sent to Cambridge, some to Oxford, some to Louvain, others to Paris, some to Orleans, others to Padua, all at the proper costs and charges of the King, which in the whole amounted to a great sum of money; and all went out of this realm besides the charge of the ambassage to those famous and notable persons of all the Universities. Especially such as bare the rule or had the custody of the University Seals were fed by the Commissioners with such great sums of money, that they did easily condescend to their requests and grant their desires. By reason whereof all the Commissioners returned with their purpose furnished according to their commissions under the Seal of every University, whereat there was no small joy conceived of the principal parties.

Insomuch that ever after the Commissioners were had in great estimation, and highly advanced and liberally rewarded far beyond their worthy deserts. Notwithstanding they prospered, and the matter went still forward, having now, as they thought, a sure staff to lean upon. These proceedings being declared unto my Lord Cardinal, he sent again for the Bishops, to whom he declared the effect of these Commissioners' labours, and for assurance thereof showed them the documents of each University under their several Seals, and the business being thus handled, they went again to consultation how things should be ordered.

At last it was concluded that it was very meet the King should send unto the Pope's Holiness the opinions of both Universities of England, and also foreign Universities, which were manifestly authorized by their common seals. And it was also thought fit that the opinions of the worthy Prelates of England should be sent to the Pope comprised in a document, which was not long time in furnishing.

Nor was it long after that the Ambassadors were assigned for this purpose, who took their journey accordingly, having certain documents, so that if the Pope would not thereupon consent to give judgment definitely in the King's case, then to require another Commission from His Holiness to be granted to his Legate to establish a Court here in England for that purpose only, to be directed to my Lord Cardinal Legate of England and to Cardinal Campeggio, Bishop of Bath (which the King gave him at a certain time when he was sent Ambassador hither from the Pope's Holiness), to determine and rightly judge according to their consciences. To which, after a long time and for the goodwill of the said Cardinal, the Pope granted their suit.

Then they returned into England, relating unto

the King their expedition, trusting that His Grace's pleasure should be now brought to pass substantially, being never more likely, considering the estate of the judges.

Long was the expectation on both sides for the coming over of the Legate from Rome, who at last arrived in England with his Commission, and being much troubled with the gout, his journey was long and tedious ere he could get to London, who should have been most solemnly received at Blackheath; but he desired not to be so entertained with pomp and vainglory, and therefore he came very privately to his own house without Temple Bar, called Bath Place, where he lodged, the house being furnished with all manner of provision of my Lord's. So after some deliberation and consultation in the ordering of the King's business now in hand by his Commission and Articles of the Ambassage, which being read, it was determined that the King and the good Queen, his lawful wife, should be judged at Bridewell and in Blackfriars, and that some place about the court should be kept for the disputation and determination of the causes and differences between the King and the Queen, who were summoned to appear before these two Legates who sat as judges, which was a strange sight and the newest device that ever was heard or read of in any story or chronicle: A King and a Queen to be compelled to appear in a court as common persons within their own realm and dominions, and to abide the judgments and decrees of their subjects, having the royal diadem and prerogative thereof.

XVI

A NEW COURT ERECTED TO DETERMINE THE KING'S CASE, TWO CARDINALS BEING JUDGES, HAVING POWER TO SUMMON THE KING AND QUEEN—THE ISSUE THEREOF

IT is a wonderful thing to consider the strength of Princes' wills when they are bent to have their pleasure fulfilled, wherein no reasonable persuasions will serve the turn. How little do they regard the dangerous sequels that may ensue as well to themselves as to their subjects! And amongst all things there is nothing that makes them more wilful than carnal love and various affecting of voluptuous desires, wherein nothing could be of greater experience than to see what inventions were furnished, what laws were enacted, what costly edifices of noble and ancient monasteries were overthrown, what diversities of opinion then arose, what extortions were then committed, how many good and learned men were then put to death, and what alterations of good ancient laws, customs and charitable foundations were turned from the relief of the poor to the utter destruction and desolation, almost to the subversion, of this noble realm.

It is a thousand pities to understand the things that since have happened to this land, the proof whereof hath taught all us Englishmen lamentable experience. If men's eyes be not blind, they may see, and if their ears be not stopped, they may hear, and if pity be not exiled, their hearts may relent and lament at the sequel of this inordinate love, although it lasted but a while. . O Lord God, withhold Thine indignation from us!

You shall understand, as I said before, that there was a court erected at Blackfriars, London, where these two Cardinals sat as judges. Now I will describe to you the order of the court. First there were many tables and benches set in manner of a consistory, one seat being higher than another for the judges aloft; above them three degrees high was a cloth of State hung and a chair royal under the same, wherein sat the King, and some distance off sat the Queen, and at the judges' feet sat the scribes and officers for the execution of the process. The chief scribe was Doctor Stevens, afterwards Bishop of Winchester, and the apparitor who was called Doctor of the Court was one Cooke of Westminster.

Then, before the King and the judges sat the Archbishop of Canterbury, Doctor Warham, and all other Bishops. There stood at both ends within counsellors learned in the spiritual laws as well on the King's as the Queen's side. Doctor Sampson, afterwards Bishop of Chichester, and Doctor Hall, afterwards Bishop of Worcester, and divers others, and proctors in the same law were Doctor Peter, who was afterwards Chief Secretary, and Doctor Tregunmill with divers others.

Now, on the other side there were Counsel for the Queen, Doctor Fisher, Bishop of Rochester, and Doctor Standish, Bishop of St. Asaph in Wales, two noble divines, especially the Bishop of Rochester, a very godly man, whose death many noble men and many worthy divines much lamented, who lost his head about this cause ere it was ended, on Tower Hill, as also another ancient doctor called Doctor Ridley, a little man but a great divine. The court being thus ordered as is before expressed, the judges commanded the Crier to proclaim silence whilst the commission was both read to the court and to the people there assembled. That done, and silence being again proclaimed, the scribes commanded the Crier to call King Henry of England, whereunto the King answered and said, 'Here!' Then called he again the Queen of England by the name of 'Katherine, Queen of England, come into the court,' etc. She made no answer thereunto, but rose immediately out of her chair where she sat, and because she could not come to the King directly by reason of the distance, therefore she came round about the court to the King and kneeled down at his feet, saying these words in broken English as followeth, viz.: 'Sir, I beseech you do me justice and right, and take some pity upon me, for I am a poor woman and a stranger, born out of your dominions, having here no indifferent Counsel and less assurance of friendship. Alas! sir, how have I offended you? what offence have I given you, intending to abridge me of life in this manner? I take God to witness I have been to you a true and loyal wife, ever conformable to your will and pleasure; never did I oppose or gainsay your mind, but always submitted myself in all things wherein you had any delight, whether it were little or much, without grudging or any sign of discontent. I have loved for your sake all men whom you have loved, whether I had cause or not, were they friends or foes. I have been your wife this twenty years, by whom you had many children, and I put it to your conscience, if there be any cause that you can allege either of dishonesty or of any other matter lawfully to put me from you, I am willing to depart with shame and rebuke; but if there be none, then I pray you let me have justice at your hands.

'The King, your father, was a man of such an excellent wit in his time that he was accounted a second Solomon, and the King of Spain, my father, Ferdinand, was taken for one of the wisest Kings that reigned in Spain these many years. So they were both wise men and noble princes, and it is no question but that they had wise counsellors of either realm as be now at this day. Who thought at the marriage of you and me to hear what new devices are now invented against me to cause me to stand to the order of this Court?

'And I conceive you do me much wrong if you condemn me for not answering, having no counsel but such as you assigned me. You must consider that they cannot be indifferent on my part, being your own subjects, and such as you have made choice of out of your own Council, whereunto they are privy and dare not disclose your pleasure.

'Therefore I most humbly beseech you to spare me until I know how my friends in Spain will advise me; but if you will not, then let your pleasure be done.'

And with that she rose, making a low curtsey to the King, and departed from thence, all the people thinking she would have returned again to her former seat; but she went presently out of the court, leaning upon the arm of one of her servants, who was her general receiver, one Mr. Griffith.

The King, seeing that she was ready to go out of the court, commanded the Crier to call her again by these words:

'Katherine, Queen of England, come into the court!'

'Lo!' quoth Mr. Griffith, 'you are called again.'

'Go on,' quoth she; 'it is no matter. It is no fit court for me, therefore I will not tarry. Go on your way.'

And so they departed, without any further answer at that time or any appearance in any other court after that.

The King, seeing she was departed thus, and considering her words, said to the audience these few words in effect:

'Forasmuch,' quoth he, 'as the Queen is gone, I will in her absence declare unto you all: She hath been to me a true, obedient wife, and as comfortable as I could wish or desire; she hath all the virtues and good qualities that belong to a woman of her dignity, or in any meaner estate. Her conditions will well declare the same.'

Then quoth my Lord Cardinal:

'I humbly beseech your Highness to declare

unto this audience whether I have been the first and chief mover of this matter unto your Highness or no, for I am much suspected of all men.'

'My Lord Cardinal,' quoth the King, 'you have rather advised me to the contrary than been any mover of the same. The special cause that moved me in this matter is a certain scruple that pricked my conscience upon certain words spoken by the Bishop of Bayonne, the French Ambassador who came hither to consult of a marriage between the Princess, our daughter, the Lady Mary, and the Duke of Orleans, second son to the King of France, and upon resolution and determination he desired respite to advertise the King his Master thereof, whether our daughter Mary should be legitimate in respect of my marriage with this woman, being some time my brother's wife, which words I pondering, begot such a scruple in my conscience that I was much troubled at it, whereby I thought myself in danger of God's heavy displeasure and indignation, and the rather because He sent us no male issue, for all the male issue that I had by my wife died immediately after they came into the world, which caused me to fear God's displeasure in that particular. Thus, my conscience being tossed in the waves of troublesome doubts, and partly in despair of having any other issue than I had by this lady, now my wife, it behoved me to consider the estate of this realm, and the danger it stands in for lack of a Prince to succeed me. I thought it therefore good, in release of this mighty burden on my conscience, as also for the quiet estate of this realm, to attempt a trial in the law herein as to whether I might lawfully take another wife without carnal concupiscence, by which God may send more issue. I have not any displeasure in the person or age of the Queen, with whom I could be well contented to continue (if our marriage may stand by the law of God) as with any woman alive, in which point consisteth all the doubt that we go about now to know by the learned wisdom of you our Prelates and Pastors of this realm and dominion now here assembled for that purpose, to whose consciences and learning I have committed the care and judgment, according to which I will (God willing) be well contented to submit myself and obey the same. And when my conscience was so troubled I moved it to you, my Lord of Lincoln, in confession, then being my ghostly father, and forasmuch as you were then in some doubt, you moved me to ask counsel of the rest of the Bishops. Whereupon I moved it to you, my Lord Cardinal, to have your licence—forasmuch as you are Metropolitan—to put this matter in question, and so I did to all you, my lords, to which you all granted under your seals, which is here to show.'

'That is truth,' quoth the Bishop of Canterbury, 'and I doubt not but my brothers will acknowledge the same.'

'No, sir; not so, under correction,' quoth the Bishop of Rochester, 'for you have not my hand and seal.'

'No?' quoth the King. 'Is not this your hand and seal?' and showed it to him in the document with seals.

'No, forsooth!' quoth the Bishop.

'How say you to that?' quoth the King to the Bishop of Canterbury.

'Sir, it is his hand,' quoth the Bishop of Canterbury.

'No, my Lord,' quoth the Bishop of Rochester. 'Indeed, you were in hand with me to have both my hand and seal, as other of the lords have done; but I answered I would never consent to any such act, for it was much against my conscience, and therefore my hand and seal shall never be set to such a document (God willing),' with many other words to that purpose.

'You say truth,' quoth the Bishop of Canterbury. 'Such words you used, but you were fully resolved at the last that I should subscribe your name and put to your seal, and you would allow of the same.'

'All which,' quoth the Bishop of Rochester, 'under correction, my lord, is untrue.'

'Well,' quoth the King, 'we will not stand in argument with you; you are but one.'

And so the King arose up, and the court was adjourned until the next day, at which time the Cardinals sat again, and the Counsel on both sides were there present to answer.

The King's Counsel alleged the matrimony not good nor lawful at the beginning, because of the carnal copulation that Prince Arthur had with the Queen.

This matter was very narrowly scanned on that side, and to prove the carnal copulation they had many reasons and similitudes of truth, and being answered negatively again on the other side, it seemed that all their former allegations were doubtful to be tried, and that no man knew.

'Yes,' quoth the Bishop of Rochester, 'I know the truth.'

'How can you know the truth,' quoth the Cardinal, 'more than any other person?'

'Yes, forsooth, my Lord,' quoth he; 'I know that God is the Truth itself, and never said but truth, and He said thus: "Quos Deus conjunxit, homo non separet." And forasmuch as this marriage was joined and made by God to a good intent, therefore I said I knew the truth, and that man cannot break any institution that God hath made and constituted.'

'So much do all faithful men know,' quoth my Lord Cardinal, 'as well as you, therefore this reason is not sufficient in this case, for the King's Counsel do allege many presumptions to prove that it was not lawful at the beginning, therefore that it was not ordained by God, for God doth nothing without a good end; therefore it is not to be doubted that if the presumptions be true, which they allege to be most true, then the conjunction neither was nor could be of God. Therefore I say unto you, my Lord of Rochester, you know not the truth, unless you can avoid their presumptions upon just reasons.'

Then quoth Dr. Ridley:

'It is a great shame and dishonour to this honourable presence that such presumptions should be alleged in this open court. No, my Lord, there belongs no reverence to this matter, for an irreverent matter may be irreverently answered.'

And so he left off, and then they proceeded to other matters. Thus passed this court from session to session and day to day, till a certain day the King sent for the Cardinal to Bridewell, who went into the Privy Chamber to him, where he was about an hour, and then departed from

NEW COURT TO DETERMINE THE KING'S CASE

the King and went to Westminster in his barge. The Bishop of Carlisle, being with him, said:

'It is a hot day to-day.'

'Yea,' quoth the Cardinal; 'if you had been as well chafed as I have been within this hour, you would say you were very hot.'

My Lord no sooner came home but he went to bed, where he had not laid two hours but my Lord of Wiltshire, Mistress Anne Boleyn's father, came to speak with him from the King. My Lord commanded he should be brought to his bedside, who told him it was the King's pleasure he should forthwith go with the Cardinal to the Queen, being then at Bridewell in her chamber, and to persuade her by their wisdom to put the whole matter into the King's own hands by her consent, which would be much better for her honour than stand to the trial at law and thereby be condemned, which would tend much to her dishonour and discredit. To perform the King's pleasure, my Lord said he was ready, and so prepared to go, but quoth he further to my Lord of Wiltshire:

'You and others of the Council have put fancies into the head of the King, whereby you trouble all the realm, but at the end you will get but small thanks both of God and the world.'

Many other words and reasons did cause my

Lord of Wiltshire to be silent, kneeling by my Lord's bedside, and at last he departed.

And then my Lord rose and took his barge, and went to Bath House to Cardinal Campeggio's, and they went together to Bridewell to the Queen's lodgings. She being in her Chamber of Presence, they told the Gentleman Usher that they came to speak with the Queen's Grace. The Queen was told the Cardinals were come to speak with her. Then she arose up, having a skein of red silk about her neck (being at work with her maids), and came to the Cardinals at the place where they awaited her coming, at whose coming quoth she:

'Alack, my Lords! I am sorry that you have attended on me so long. What is your pleasure with me?'

'If it please your Grace,' quoth the Cardinal, 'to go to your Privy Chamber, we will show you the cause of our coming.'

'My Lord,' said she, 'if you have anything to say to me, say it openly before all these folk, for I fear nothing that you can say to me or against me; but I am willing all the world should both see and hear it, and therefore speak your minds openly.'

Then began my Lord to speak to her in Latin.

'Nay, good my Lord, speak to me in English,' quoth she, 'although I do understand some Latin.'

'Forsooth,' quoth my Lord. 'Good madam, if it please your Grace, we come both to know your mind, what you are disposed to do in this matter, and also to declare to you secretly our counsels and opinions, which we do for very zeal and obedience to your Grace.'

'My Lords,' quoth she, 'I thank you for your good will, but to make answer to your requests, I cannot so suddenly, for I was sitting amongst my maids at work, little thinking of any such matter, wherein is requisite some deliberation and a better head than mine to answer, for I need counsel in this case which concerns me so nearly, and friends here I have none. They are in Spain, in mine own country. Also, my Lords, I am a poor woman of too weak capacity to answer such noble persons of wisdom as you are, in so weighty a matter. And therefore be good to me, a woman destitute of friendship here in a foreign region, and your counsel I also shall be glad to hear.' And therewith she took my Lord by the hand and led him into her Privy Chamber, where they stayed awhile, and I heard her voice loud, but what she said I know not.

This done, they went to the King and made a relation unto him of the passages between the Queen and them, and so they departed.

This strange case proceeded and went forwards

from court day to court day, until it came to that time that every man expected to hear judgment given, at which time all their proceedings were openly read in Latin. That done, the King's Counsel at the Bar moved for judgment. Quoth Cardinal Campeggio: 'I will not give judgment till I have related the whole proceedings to the Pope, whose counsel and commandment I will in this case observe. The matter is too high for us to give hasty judgment, considering the persons and the doubtful occasions alleged, and also whose Commissioners we are, by whose authority we sit. It is good reason therefore that we make our Chief Lord counsel in the same before we proceed to definite judgment. I came not to please for any favour, reward or fear of any person alive, be he King or otherwise; I have no such respect to the person that I should offend my conscience. And the party defendant will make no answer here, but rather doth appeal from us. I am an old man, both weak and sickly, and look every day for death; what shall it avail me to put my soul in danger of God's displeasure, to my utter damnation, for the favour of any prince in this world? My being here is only to see justice administered according to my conscience.

'The defendant supposeth that we be not indifferent judges, considering the King's high dignity, and authority within his realm. And we being both his subjects, she thinks we will not do her justice, and therefore to avoid all these ambiguities I adjourn the court for the time according to the Court of Rome, from whence our jurisdiction is derived; for if we should go further than our commission doth warrant us, it were but a folly and blameworthy, because we shall be breakers of the Orders from whom we have, as I said, our authority derived.'

And so the court was dissolved, and no more was done.

Thereupon, by the King's commandment, stepped up the Duke of Suffolk, and with a haughty countenance uttered these words: 'It was never thus in England until we had Cardinals amongst us.' These words were set forth with such vehemence that all men marvelled what he intended, the Duke further expressing some opprobrious words.

My Lord Cardinal, perceiving his vehemence, soberly said: 'Sir, of all men in this realm you have least cause to malign Cardinals, for if I, poor Cardinal, had not been, you should not at this present have had a head upon your shoulders wherewith to make such a bray in dispute of us, who wish you no harm, neither have given you such cause to be offended with us. I would have you think, my Lord, I and my brother wish the

King as much happiness and the realm as much honour, wealth and peace as you or any other subject of whatsoever degree he be within this realm, and would as gladly accomplish his lawful desires. And now, my Lord, I pray you show me what you would do in such a case as this, if you were one of the King's Commissioners in a foreign region about some weighty matter, the solution whereof was very doubtful to be decided. Would you not advertise the King's Majesty ere you went through with the same? I doubt not but you would, and therefore abate your malice and spite, and consider we are Commissioners for a time, and cannot by virtue of a Commission proceed to judgment without the knowledge and consent of the chief authority, and without license obtained from him who is the Pope. Therefore do we neither more nor less than our Commission allows us, and if any man will be offended with us, he is an unwise man. Therefore pacify yourself, my Lord, and speak like a man of honour and wisdom, or hold your peace. Speak not reproachfully of your friends; you best know what friendship I have shown you. I never did reveal it to any person till now, either to mine own praise or your dishonour.'

Whereupon the Duke went his way and said no more, being much discontented.

This matter continued thus a long season, and the King was in displeasure against my Lord Cardinal, because his suit had no better success to his purpose. Notwithstanding, the Cardinal excused himself by his Commission, which gave him no authority to proceed to judgment without the knowledge of the Pope, who reserved the same to himself. At last they were advertised by a post that they should take deliberation in the matter until his Council were opened, which should not be till Bartholomew-tide next.

The King, thinking it would be too long ere it would be determined, sent an ambassador to the Pope, to persuade him to show so much favour to His Majesty as that it might be sooner determined.

On this ambassage went Dr. Stephen Gardiner, then called by the name of Doctor Steven, Secretary to the King, afterwards Bishop of Winchester. This ambassador stayed there till the latter end of summer, of whose return you shall hereafter hear.

XVII

OF CERTAIN PASSAGES CONDUCING TO THE CARDINAL'S FALL

NOW, the King commanded the Queen to be removed from the Court and sent to another place, and presently after the King rode on progress and had in his company Mistress Anne Boleyn, in which time Cardinal Campeggio asked to be discharged and sent home to Rome; and in the interim returned Mr. Secretary, and it was concluded that my Lord should come to the King to Grafton in Northamptonshire, as also Cardinal Campeggio, being a stranger, should be conducted thither by my Lord Cardinal. And so the next Sunday there were divers opinions that the King should not speak with my Lord; whereupon there were many great wagers laid.

These two Prelates being come to the Court, and alighting, expected to be received of the great officers, as the manner was, but they found the contrary. Nevertheless, because the Cardinal Campeggio was a stranger, the officers met him with staves in their hands in the outer court, and so conveyed him to his lodging prepared for him; and after my Lord had brought him to his lodging, he departed, thinking to have gone to his chamber as he was wont to do. But it was told him that he had no lodging or chamber appointed for him in the Court, which news did much astonish him. Sir Henry Norris, who was then Groom of the Stole, came unto him and desired him to take his chamber for awhile until another was provided for him.

'For I assure you,' quoth he, 'here is but little room in this house for the King, and therefore I humbly beseech your Grace accept of mine for a season.'

My Lord, thanking him for his courtesy, went to his chamber, where he shifted his riding apparel.

In the meantime came divers noblemen of his friends to welcome him to the Court, by whom my Lord was advertised of all things touching the King's favour or displeasure, and being thus informed of the cause thereof, he was the more able to excuse himself. So my Lord made him ready and went to the Chamber of Presence with the other Cardinal, where the Lords of the Council stood all in a row in order in the chamber, and all the Lords saluted them both. And there were present many gentlemen who came on purpose to see the meeting and countenance of the King to my Lord Cardinal. Then immediately after the King came into the Chamber of Presence, standing under the cloth of State.

Then my Lord Cardinal took Cardinal Campeggio by the hand and knelt down before the King, but what he said unto him I know not, but his countenance was amiable, and His Majesty stooped down, and with both hands took him up, and then took him by the hand and went to the window with him, and talked with him a good while.

Then to have beheld the countenance of the Lords and noblemen that had laid wagers, it would have made you smile, especially those that had laid their money that the King would not speak with him.

Thus were they deceived, for the King was in earnest discourse with him, insomuch that I heard the King say, 'How can this be? Is not this your hand?' and pulled a letter out of his own bosom, and showed the same to my Lord. And as I perceived, my Lord so answered the same that the King had no more to say, but said to my Lord Cardinal:

'Go to your dinner, and take my Lord Cardinal to keep you company, and after dinner I will speak further with you.'

And so they departed, and the King that day dined with Mistress Anne Boleyn in her chamber.

Then there was set up in the Presence Chamber a table for my Lord and other Lords of the Council, where they dined together, and sat at dinner telling of divers matters.

'The King should do well,' quoth my Lord Cardinal, 'to send his Bishops and Chaplains home to their cures and benefices.'

'Yea, marry,' quoth my Lord of Norfolk, 'and so it were meet for you to do also.'

'I would be well contented therewith,' quoth my Lord, 'if it were the King's pleasure, and with His Grace's leave to go to my cure at Winchester.'

'Nay,' quoth my Lord of Norfolk, 'to your benefice at York, where your greatest honour and charge is.'

'Even as it shall please the King,' quoth my Lord Cardinal.

And so they fell upon other discourses. For, indeed, the nobility were loath he should be so near the King as to continue at Winchester. Immediately after dinner they fell to counsel till the waiters had also dined.

I heard it reported by those that waited on the

King at dinner, that Mistress Anne Boleyn was offended as much as she dared, that the King did so graciously entertain my Lord Cardinal, saying:

'Sir, is it not a marvellous thing to see into what great debt and danger he hath brought you with all your subjects?'

'How so?' quoth the King.

'Forsooth,' quoth she, 'there is not a man in all your whole realm of England worth a hundred pounds, but he hath indebted you to him' (meaning of loan which the King had of his subjects).

'Well, well,' quoth the King, 'for that matter there was no blame in him, for I know that matter better than you or any else.'

'Nay,' quoth she, 'besides that, what exploits hath he wrought in several parts and places of this realm to your great slander and disgrace! There is never a nobleman but if he had done half so much as he hath done, were well worthy to lose his head. Yea, if my Lord of Norfolk, my Lord of Suffolk, my father or any other man had done much less than he hath done, they should have lost their heads ere this.'

'Then, I perceive,' quoth the King, 'you are none of my Lord Cardinal's friends.'

'Why, sir,' quoth she, 'I have no cause nor any that love you, no more hath your Grace, if you did well consider his indirect and unlawful doings.'

By that time the waiters had dined and were taking up the table, and so for that time ended their communication. You may perceive by this how the old malice was not forgotten, but began to kindle and be set on fire, which was stirred by the Cardinal's ancient enemies whom I have before mentioned in this treatise.

The King for that time departed from Mistress Anne Boleyn, and came to the Chamber of Presence and called for my Lord, and in the great window had a long discourse with him, but of what I know not. Afterwards the King took him by the hand and led him into the Privy Chamber, and sat in consultation with him all alone without any other of the Lords, till it was dark night, which troubled all his enemies very sore, who had no other way but by Mistress Anne Boleyn, in whom was all their trust and confidence for the accomplishment of their enterprises, for without her they feared all their purposes would be frustrated.

Now, at night was warning given me that there was no room for my Lord to lodge in the Court, so that I was forced to provide my Lord a lodging in the country about Easton, at one Mr. Empston's house, where my Lord came to supper by torchlight, it being late before my Lord parted from the King, who willed him to resort to him in the morning, for that he would talk further with him about the same matter; and in the morning my Lord came again, at whose coming the King's Majesty was ready to ride, desiring my Lord to consult with the Lords in his absence, and saying he would not talk with him. He commanded my Lord to depart with Cardinal Campeggio, who had already taken his leave of the King.

This sudden departure of the King was the special work of Mistress Anne Boleyn, who rode with him purposely to draw him away, so that he might not return till after the departure of the Cardinals.

So my Lord rode away after dinner with Cardinal Campeggio, who took his journey towards Rome with the King's reward, but what it was I am not certain. After their departure it was told the King that Cardinal Campeggio was departed, and had great treasure with him of my Lord Cardinal's to be conveyed in great amount to Rome, whither they surmised he would secretly repair out of this realm. Insomuch that they caused a post to ride after the Cardinal to search him, who overtook him at Calais and detained him till search was made, but there was found no more than was received of the King for a reward.

Now, after Cardinal Campeggio was gone, Michaelmas Term drew on, against which my Lord Cardinal repaired to his house at Westminster; and when the Term began, he went into the Hall in such manner as he was accustomed to do and sat in the Chancery, being then Lord Chancellor of England. After this day he never sat more. The next day he stayed at home for the coming of the Lords of Norfolk and Suffolk, who came not that day but the next, and did then declare unto my Lord that it was the King's pleasure that he should surrender up the Great Seal of England into their hands, and that he should depart unto Asher, which is a house near unto Hampton Court belonging to the Bishopric of Winchester.

The Cardinal demanded of them to see their commission that gave them such authority. They answered that they were sufficient Commissioners, and had authority to do no less from the King's own mouth. Notwithstanding, he would in nowise agree to their demand without further knowledge of their authority, telling them that the Great Seal was delivered to him by the King's own person, to enjoy the ministration thereof, together with the Chancellorship during the term of his life, whereof for surety he had the King's Letters Patent to show. This matter was much debated between him and the Dukes, with many angry words, which he took patiently, insomuch that the Dukes were obliged to depart without their purpose at that time, and returned to Windsor to the King, and the next day they returned to my Lord with the King's Letters. Whereupon, in obedience to the King's command, my Lord delivered to them the Broad Seal, which they brought to Windsor to the King.

Then my Lord called his officers before him and took account of all things they had in their charge, and in his gallery were set divers tables, upon which were laid divers and great store of rich stuffs, as whole pieces of silk of all colours, velvets, satins, damask, taffeta, grograine, scarlets and divers rich commodities. Also there were a thousand pieces of fine holland. The hangings of the gallery were cloth of gold and cloth of silver and rich cloth of baudkin of divers colours, which were hung in expectation of the King's coming. Also on one side of the gallery were hung rich suits of copes of his own provision, which were made for the colleges at Oxford and Ipswich; they were the richest that ever I saw in all my life.

Then had he two chambers adjoining the gallery, the one most commonly called the Gilt Chamber, the other the Council Chamber, wherein were set two broad and long tables, whereupon was set such abundance of plate of all sorts as was almost incredible. A great part were all of clean gold, and upon every table and cupboard where the plate was set were books reporting every kind of plate and every piece, with the contents and the weight thereof.

Thus were all things furnished and prepared, and he gave the charge of the said stuff, with other things remaining in every office, to be delivered to the King as he gave charge. All things being ordered as is before rehearsed, my Lord prepared to depart, and resolved to go by water. But before his going, Sir W. Gascoigne, being his treasurer, came unto him, and said:

'Sir, I am sorry for your Grace, for I hear you are to go straight to the Tower.'

'Is this the best comfort,' quoth my Lord, 'you can give to your master in adversity? It hath always been your inclination to be light of credit, and much lighter in reporting of lies. I would you should know, Sir William, and all those reporters too, that it is untrue, for I never deserved to come there. Although it hath pleased the King to take my house ready furnished for his pleasure, at this time I would all the world should know that I have nothing but it is of right from him, and of him I received all that I have. It is therefore convenient and reason that I tender the same to him again.'

Then my Lord, with his train of gentlemen and

yeomen, which was no small company, took his barge at his private stairs and went by water to Putney, at which time upon the water were abundance of boats filled with people, expecting to have seen my Lord Cardinal go to the Tower, which they longed to see. O wondering and new-fangled world! Is it not a time to consider the mutability of this uncertain world? For the common people ever desire things for the sake of novelty which after turn to their small profit and advantage. For if you mark the sequel, they had small cause to rejoice at his fall. I cannot but see that all men in favour are envied by the common people, though they do minister justice truly.

Thus continued my Lord at Asher three or four weeks without either beds, sheets, tablecloths, or dishes to eat their meat in, or wherewith to buy any. But there was good store of all kinds of victuals, and of beer and wine plenty, but afterwards my Lord borrowed some plate and dishes of the Bishop of Carlisle. Thus continued my Lord in this strange state till after All-hallown tide, and being one day at dinner Mr. Cromwell told him he ought in conscience to consider the true and good service that he and other of his servants had done who never forsook him in weal and woe. Then quoth my Lord:

'Alas! Tom, you know I have nothing to give

you nor them, which makes me both ashamed and sorry that I have nothing to requite your faithful services.' Whereupon Mr. Cromwell told my Lord that 'he had abundance of chaplains that were preferred by his Grace to benefices of some thousand pounds, and others five hundred pounds, some more, some less, and we, your poor servants, take more pains in one day's service than all your idle chaplains have done in a year. Therefore, if they will not impart liberally to you in your great indigence, it is a pity they should live, and all the world will have them in indignation for their great ingratitude to their master.'

Afterwards my Lord commanded me to call all his gentlemen and yeomen up into the great chamber, commanding all the gentlemen to stand on the right hand and the yeomen on the left. At last my Lord came out in his rochet upon a violet gown like a bishop's, who went with his chaplains to the upper end of the chamber, where was a great window. Beholding his goodly number of servants, he could not speak to them, while the tears ran down his cheeks, which being perceived by the servants, caused fountains of tears to gush out of their sorrowful eyes in such sort as to cause my heart to lament. At last my Lord spoke to them to this effect and purpose, saying:

'Most faithful gentlemen and true-hearted yeomen, I much lament that in prosperity I did not do so much for you as I might have done and was in my power to do. I consider that if in my prosperity I should have commended you to the King then I should have incurred the displeasure of the King's servants, who would not spare to report behind my back that there could escape the Cardinal and his servants no office in the Court, and by that means I should have run into open slander of all the world; but now it is come to pass that it hath pleased the King to take all that I have into his hands, so that I have now nothing to give you, for I have nothing left me but the bare clothes on my back.'

So he, giving them all hearty thanks, went away, and afterwards many of his servants departed from him, some to their wives, some to their friends, Master Cromwell to London, it being then the beginning of Parliament.

CHAPTER XVIII

THE CARDINAL IS ACCUSED OF HIGH TREASON IN THE PARLIAMENT HOUSE, AGAINST WHICH ACCUSATION MR. CROMWELL (LATE SERVANT TO HIM), BEING A BURGESS IN THE PARLIAMENT, MADE DEFENCE

THE aforesaid Master Cromwell, after his departure from my Lord, devised with himself to be one of the Burgesses of the Parliament. Being in London, he chanced to meet one Sir Thomas Russell, Knight, a special friend of his, whose son was one of the Burgesses of the Parliament, of whom he obtained his room, and by that means put his foot into the Parliament House. Three days after his departure from my Lord he came again to Asher, and I being there with my Lord, he said unto me with a pleasant countenance:

'I have adventured my feet where I will be better regarded ere the Parliament be dissolved.'

And after he had some talk with my Lord, he made haste to London, because he would not be absent from the Parliament, to the intent he might acquaint my Lord what was there objected against him, thereby the better to make his defence, insomuch that there was nothing at any time objected against my Lord but he was ready to make answer thereunto. Being thus earnest in his master's behalf, he was reputed the most faithful servant to his master of all others, and was generally of all men highly commended.

Then was there brought a Bill of Articles into the Parliament House to have my Lord condemned of high treason, against which Master Cromwell did inveigh, so discreetly and with such witty persuasions, that the same would take no effect. Then were his enemies constrained to indict him of a Præmunire, to entitle the King to all his goods and possessions which he had obtained and purchased for the maintenance of his Colleges of Oxford and Ipswich, which were both most sumptuous buildings. To the Judges that were sent to take my Lord's answer herein he thus answered:

'My Lord Judges, the King knoweth whether I have offended or no in using my prerogative, for the which I am indicted. I have the King's license in my coffer, under his hand and Broad Seal, for the executing and using thereof in most large manner, the which now are in the hands of mine enemies. Therefore, because I will not here stand to contend with His Majesty in his own case, I will here presently before you confess the indictment, and put myself wholly at the mercy and grace of the King, trusting that he hath a conscience and reason to consider the truth, and my humble submission and obedience wherein I might well stand to my trial with justice. Thus much may you say to His Highness, that I wholly submit myself under his obedience in all things to his princely will and pleasure, whom I never disobeyed or repugned, but was always contented and glad to please him before God, whom I ought most chiefly to have believed and obeyed, which I now repent. I most heartily desire you to have me commended to him, for whom I shall, during my life, pray to God to send him much prosperity, honour, and victory over his enemies.'

And so they left him.

After this Mr. Shelley, the Judge, was sent to speak with my Lord, who understanding he had come, issued out of his Privy Chamber and came to him to know his business. He, after due salutation, did declare unto him that the King's pleasure was to demand my Lord's house, called York Place, near Westminster, belonging to the Bishopric of York, and to possess the same according to the laws of his realm.

'His Highness hath sent for all his Judges and learned Counsel to know their opinions for your assurance thereof, who be fully resolved that your Grace must make a recognition, and before a Judge acknowledge and confess the right thereof to belong to the King and his successors, and so His Highness shall be assured thereof.

'Wherefore it hath pleased the King to send me hither to take of you the recognizance, having in your Grace such confidence that you will not refuse to do so; therefore I do desire to know your Grace's pleasure therein.'

'Master Shelley,' quoth my Lord, 'I know the King of his own nature is a royal spirit, not requiring more than reason shall lead him to by the law. And therefore I counsel you and all other Judges and learned men of his Council to put no more into his head than law, that may stand with conscience, for when you tell him that this is law, it were well done you should tell him that, although this is law, yet it is not conscience; for law without conscience is not good to be ministered by a King or his Council nor by any of his ministers, for every Council to a King ought to have respect to conscience before the rigour of the law, for "laus est facere quod decet non quod licet." The King ought for his royal dignity and prerogative to mitigate the rigour of the law, and therefore in his princely place he hath constituted a Chancellor to order for him the same, and therefore the Court of Chancery hath been commonly called the Court of Conscience, for that it hath jurisdiction to command the law in every case to desist from the rigour of the execution. And now I say to you, Master Shelley, have I a power or may I with conscience give that away which is now mine for me and my successors? If this be law and conscience, I pray you show me your opinion.'

'Forsooth,' quoth he, 'there is no great conscience in it, but having regard to the King's great power, it may the better stand with conscience, who is sufficient to recompense the Church of York with the double value.'

'That I know well,' quoth my Lord; 'but there is no such condition, but only a bare and simple seizure of another's right; if every Bishop should do so, then might every Prelate give away the patrimony of the Church, and so in process of time leave nothing for their successors to maintain their dignities, which would be but little to the King's honour. Well,' quoth my Lord, 'let me see your commission,' which was shown to him. 'Then,' quoth my Lord, ' tell His Highness that I am his most faithful subject and obedient beadsman, whose command I will in no wise disobey, but will in all things fulfil his pleasure, as you, the fathers of the law, say I may. Therefore I charge your conscience to discharge me, and show His Highness from me, that I must desire His Majesty to remember there is both Heaven and Hell.'

And thereupon the clerk took and wrote the recognizance, and after some secret talk they departed.

Thus continued my Lord at Asher, receiving daily messages from the Court, some good, some bad, but more ill than good, for his enemies, perceiving the good affection the King always bore towards him, devised a means to disquiet his patience, thinking thereby to give him occasion to fret and chafe, that death should rather ensue than increase of health or life, which they most desired, for they feared him more after his fall than they did in prosperity, fearing that he should, by reason of the King's favour, rise again and be again in favour and great at the Court; for then they his enemies might be in danger of their lives for their cruelty wrongfully ministered unto him, and by their malicious surmises invented and brought to pass against him. Therefore they did continually find new matters against him to vex him and make him fret, but he was a wise man and did arm himself with much patience.

At Christmas he fell very sore sick, most likely to die. The King, hearing thereof, was very sorry and sent Dr. Butts, his physician, unto him, who found him very dangerously sick in bed, and returned to the King. The King demanded, saying:

'Have you seen yonder man?'

'Yes, sir,' quoth he.

'How do you find him?' quoth the King.

'Sir,' quoth he, 'if you will have him dead, I will warrant you he will be dead within these four days, if he receive no comfort from you shortly.'

'Marry, God forbid,' quoth the King, 'that he should die, for I would not lose him for twenty thousand pounds. I pray you go to him and do your cure upon him.'

'Then must your Grace send him some comfortable message,' quoth Dr. Butts.

'So I will by you,' quoth the King; 'therefore make speed to him again and you shall deliver him this ring from me for a token' (in the which ring was engraved the King's image with a ruby, as like the King as was possible to be devised). 'This ring he knoweth well, for he gave me the same, and tell him that I am not offended with him in my heart for anything, and that shall be known shortly; therefore bid him pluck up his heart and be of good comfort. And I charge you come not from him till you have brought him out of the danger of death, if it be possible.'

Then spake the King to Mistress Anne Boleyn:

'Good sweetheart, as you love me send the Cardinal a token at my request, and in so doing you shall deserve our thanks.'

She being disposed not to offend the King, would not disobey his loving request, but took immediately her tablet of gold that hung at her side, and delivered it to Dr. Butts, with very gentle and loving words. And so he departed to Asher with speed, and after him the King sent Dr. Cromer, Dr. Clement, and Dr. Wotton, to consult and advise with Dr. Butts for my Lord's recovery.

Now, after Dr. Butts had been with him and delivered him the tokens from the King and Mistress Anne Boleyn, with the most comfortable words he could devise on the King's and Mistress Anne's behalf, he raised himself in his bed and received the tokens very joyfully, giving him many thanks for his trouble and good comfort. Dr. Butts told him further that the King's pleasure was that he should minister unto him for his health, and for the better and more assured ways he hath also sent Dr. Cromer, Dr. Clement and Dr. Wotton, all to join for his recovery.

THE CARDINAL ACCUSED OF HIGH TREASON 157

'Therefore, my Lord,' quoth Dr. Butts, 'it were well they were called to visit you, and to consult for your disease.'

At which my Lord was contented, and sent for them to hear their judgments, but he trusted more to Dr. Cromer than all the rest, because he was the very means of bringing him from Paris to England and of giving him partly his exhibition in Paris.

To be short, in four days they set him again upon his feet, and got him a good stomach to his meat.

All this done and my Lord in a right good way of amendment, they took their leaves and departed, to whom my Lord offered his reward, but they refused, saying the King had given a special commandment that they should take nothing of him, for at their return he would reward them of his own cost.

After this my Lord continued at Asher till Candlemas, before and against which feast the King caused to be sent to my Lord three or four loads of stuff, and most thereof, except beds and kitchen-stuff, was loaded in standards, wherein was both plate and rich hangings and chapel stuff, which was done without the knowledge of the Lords of the Council, for all which he rendered the King most humble and hearty thanks, and afterwards he made suit unto the King to be removed from Asher to Richmond, which request was granted.

The house of Richmond a little before was repaired by my Lord to his great cost, for the King had made an exchange with him for Hampton Court. Had the Lords of the Council known of these favours from the King to the Cardinal, they would have persuaded the King to the contrary, for they feared lest his present abode near the King might move the King at some season to resort unto him, and to call him home again, considering the great and daily affection the King bore unto him. Therefore they moved the King that my Lord might go down to the north to his benefice there, where he might be a good stay, as they alleged, to the country, to which the King condescended, thinking no less but that all had been true according as they had related, being with such seriousness that the King was straightway persuaded to their conclusion.

Thereupon my Lord of Norfolk told Master Cromwell, who daily did resort to my Lord, that he should say to him that he must go home to his benefice.

'Well, then, Thomas,' quoth my Lord, 'we will go to Winchester.'

THE CARDINAL ACCUSED OF HIGH TREASON 159

'I will, then,' quoth Master Cromwell, 'tell my Lord of Norfolk what you say;' and so he did at his next meeting of him.

'What should he do there?' quoth the Duke. 'Let him go to the rich Bishopric of York, where his greatest honour and charge lieth.'

The Lords who were not his friends, perceiving that my Lord was disposed to plant himself so nigh the King, thought then to withdraw his appetite from Winchester, and moved the King to give my Lord a pension of 4,000 marks out of Winchester, and to distribute all the rest amongst the nobility and his servants, and so likewise to divide the revenues of St. Albans, whereof some had two hundred pounds. All the revenues of his lands belonging to his College at Oxford and Ipswich the King took into his own hands, whereof Master Cromwell had the government by my Lord's assignment, and it was thought very necessary that he should have the same still who executed all things so well and exactly, that he was had in great estimation for his behaviour therein.

Now, it came to pass that any annuities or fees given by the King for term of life or by patent could not be good but only for and during my Lord's life, forasmuch as the King had no longer estate therein, but what he had by my Lord's attainder in the Præmunire; and to make their estate good and sufficient there was no other way but to obtain my Lord's confirmation of their patents. To bring this about there was no other means but by Master Cromwell, who was thought the fittest instrument for this purpose, and for his pains therein he was worthily rewarded, and his demeanour, his honesty and wisdom was such that the King took great notice of him, as you shall hereafter hear.

Still, the Lords thought long till my Lord was removed further off from the King, wherefore, among others of the Lords, my Lord of Norfolk said:

'Master Cromwell, methinks the Cardinal thy master makes no haste to go northwards. Tell him, if he go not away, I will tear him with my teeth. Therefore I would advise him to prepare with speed, or I will set him forwards.'

These words reported Mr. Cromwell to my Lord at his next visit, which was to Richmond, the Cardinal having obtained license of the King to remove from Asher to Richmond. In the evening, being accustomed to walk in the garden, and I being with him standing in an alley, I espied certain images of beasts counterfeited in timber, which I went nearer to take the better view of them. Among them I saw standing a dun cow, at which I mused most of all. My Lord then suddenly came to me unawares, and speaking to me, said:

'What have you spied there whereat you look so earnestly?'

'Forsooth,' quoth I, 'if it please your Grace, I here behold these images which I suppose were ordained to be set up in the King's palace, but amongst them all I have most considered this cow, which seems to me the artificer's masterpiece.'

'Yea, marry,' quoth my Lord, 'upon this cow there hangs a certain prophecy which perhaps you never heard of. There is a saying that

>'"When the cow doth ride the bull,
>Then, priest, beware thy skull,"'

of which saying neither my Lord, that declared it, nor I, that heard it, understood the meaning, although the prophecy was then working to be brought to pass. This cow the King gave as one of his beasts appertaining from antiquity unto his earldom of Richmond, which was his ancient inheritance. This prophecy was afterwards expounded in this manner. The dun cow, because it is the King's beast, betokens the King, and the bull Mistress Anne Boleyn, who after was Queen, because that her father gave the same beast in his cognizance, so that when the King had married Queen Anne the prophecy was thought of all men to be fulfilled, for what a number of priests, religious and seculars, lost their heads for offending of those laws made to bring this matter to pass is not unknown to all the world, therefore it may well be judged that this prophecy is fulfilled.

You have heard what words the Duke of Norfolk spoke to Master Cromwell touching my Lord's going into the north. Then said my Lord:

'Thomas, it is time to be going, therefore I pray you go to the King and tell him I would go to my benefice at York but for lack of money, and desire his Grace to help me to some, for you may say the last money I had from his Grace was too little to pay my debts, and to compel me to pay the rest of my debts is too much extremity, seeing all my goods are taken from me. Also show my Lord of Norfolk and the rest of the Council that I would depart if I had money.'

'Sir,' quoth Master Cromwell, 'I shall do my best.'

And so, after other communication, departed, and came to London. Then at the beginning of Lent my Lord removed his lodging into the Charterhouse at Richmond, where he lay in a lodging that Dr. Collet made for himself, and every afternoon for the time of his residence there would he sit in contemplation with some one of the most ancient Fathers there, who converted him to despise the vainglory of this world, and there they gave unto him shirts of hair to wear next his body, which he wore divers time after.

The Lords assigned that my Lord should have 1,000 marks pension out of Winchester for his going down into the north, which, when the King heard of, he commanded it should be forthwith paid unto Master Cromwell. And the King commanded Master Cromwell to repair to him again when he had received the said sum, which accordingly he did, to whom His Majesty said:

'Show your Lord that I have sent him £10,000 of my benevolence, and tell him he shall not lack; bid him be of good comfort.'

Master Cromwell, on my Lord's behalf, thanked the King for his royal liberality towards my Lord, and with that departed and delivered the money and joyful tidings to the Cardinal at Richmond, wherein my Lord did not a little rejoice. Forthwith there was preparation made for his going. He had with him in his train 150 persons and twelve carts to carry his goods, which he sent from his college at Oxford, besides other carts for the carriage of his necessaries for his buildings. He kept his solemn feast of Easter at Peterborough, and upon Palm Sunday he bore his palm and went in procession with the monks, and upon Thursday he made his Maundy, having fifty poor men, whose feet he washed and kissed, and after he had dried them, he gave every one of them twelve pence and three ells of good canvas to make them shirts, and each of them had a pair of new shoes and a cask of red herrings. Upon Easter Day he rode to the Resurrection, and that day he went in procession in his Cardinal's vestments, and having his hat on his head, and sung the High Mass there himself solemnly. After his Mass he gave his benediction to all the hearers, and clean remission. From Peterborough he took his journey into the north, but made some stay by the way, and many things happened in his journey too tedious here to relate. At the last he came to Scroby, where he continued till Michaelmas, exercising many deeds of charity. Most commonly every Sunday, if the weather served, would he go to some poor parish church thereabouts, and there would say the Divine Service, and either said or heard Mass, and then caused one of his Chaplains to preach the Word of God to the people, and afterwards he would dine in some honest house in the town, where was distributed to the poor alms as well of meat and drink, and money to supply the want of meat and drink if the number of poor did exceed. About Michaelmas next he removed from thence to

Cawood Castle, within seven miles of the city of York, where we had much honour and love from all men, high and low, and where he kept a plentiful house for all comers. Also he built and repaired the Castle, which was much decayed, having at the least 300 persons daily in work to whom he paid wages. And while there all the Doctors and Prebends of the Church of York did repair to my Lord according to their duties, as unto the chief head, patron and father of their spiritual dignities, who did joyfully welcome him into those parts, saying it was no small comfort unto them to see their Head among them, who had been so long absent from them, being all that while like fatherless and comfortless children for want of his presence, and that they trusted shortly to see him amongst them in his own church—to whom he made answer that it was the especial cause of his coming to be amongst them as a father and a natural brother.

'Sir,' quoth they, 'you must understand the ordinances and rules of our Church, whereof, although you be the head and sole governor, yet you are not so well acquainted as we be therein. Therefore, if it please your Grace, we shall (under favour) open unto you some part of the ancient laws of our Church. The old law and custom hath been that our head Prelate and Pastor, as you now are, may not come above our choir door, until by due order he be installed. Nor if you should happen to die before your installation, you should not be buried above in the choir, but in the body of the church beneath. Therefore, we humbly desire and beseech you, in the name of all our brethren, that you would vouchsafe to do therein, as our ancient Fathers, your predecessors, have done, and that you would not break the laudable customs of our Church, to the which we are obliged by oath at our first admittance to observe with divers others, which in our Chapter doth remain upon record.'

'These records,' quoth my Lord, 'would I fain see, and then you shall know further of my advice and mind in this business.'

A day was fixed to bring their records to my Lord, at which time they resorted to my Lord with their register and books of records, wherein were fairly written their institutions and rules, which every minister of their Church was most principally and chiefly bound to observe and safely keep and maintain.

When my Lord had read the records he determined to be at the Cathedral Church of York the next Monday after All-hallown-tide, against which time due preparation was made for the same, but not in so sumptuous a manner as was done for his predecessors before him, nor yet in such sort as the fame and common report was afterwards made of him, to his great slander. I myself was sent by my Lord of York to see that all things there should be ordered and provided for that solemnity in a very decent form, to the honour of that ancient and worthy monastery of York.

It came to pass that upon All-hallows Day one of the head and principal officers of the said Cathedral Church, which should have had most doing at my Lord's installation, was with my Lord at Cawood, and sitting at dinner, they fell into communication of this matter, and the order and ceremony thereof, he saying that my Lord Cardinal should go on foot from a chapel which stands without the gates of the city, called St. James's Chapel, unto the minster, upon cloth, which should be distributed to the poor after his said passage to the church. My Lord hearing this, replied and said:

'Although perhaps our predecessors have gone upon cloth, yet we intend to go on foot without any such pomp or glory.' And therefore he gave order to his servants to go as humbly thither as might be, without any sumptuous apparel. 'For,' said he, 'I intend to come to you on Sunday to be installed, and to make but one dinner for you at the close, and the next day to dine with the Mayor, and so return hither again.'

The day being not unknown to all the country, the gentlemen, Abbots, and Priors sent such provision in that it was almost incredible for store and variety. The common people held my Lord in great estimation for his purity and liberality, and also for his familiar manners and good behaviour amongst them, and by means thereof he gained much love of all the people in the northern parts of England.

XIX

OF THE CARDINAL'S FALL, AND HOW HE WAS ARRESTED OF HIGH TREASON

WHAT happened before his last troubles at Cawood is a sign or token from God of that which should follow. I will now declare, God willing, how my Lord's enemies, being then at the Court about the King in good estimation and honourable dignities—how, seeing now my Lord in great favour, and fearing the King would now call him home again, they therefore did plot among themselves to despatch him by means of some sinister treason, or to bring him into the King's indignation by some other means.

This was their daily study and consultation, having for their especial help and furtherance as many vigilant attendants upon him as the poets say Argus had eyes.

The King with these their continual complaints was moved to much indignation, and thought it good that the Cardinal should come up and to stand trial in his own person, which his enemies did not like, notwithstanding he was sent for, and after this sort.

First they devised that Sir Walter Walshe, Knight, one of the King's Privy Chamber, should be sent down with a commission into the north, and the Earl of Northumberland, who was sometime brought up in the house of my Lord, being joined in commission with him, should arrest my Lord of high treason. This being resolved on, Sir Walter Walshe prepared for his journey with his commission and certain documents annexed to the same, and took horse at the Court gate upon Allhallows Day towards my Lord of Northumberland. Now I will declare what I promised before concerning a sign or token of the trouble that ensued for my Lord.

Upon All-hallows Day my Lord was sitting at dinner, having at his board divers of his Chaplains to bear him company for want of other guests. You shall now understand that my Lord's great cross which stood by fell, and in the fall broke Doctor Bonner's head, insomuch that some blood ran down. My Lord, perceiving the fall thereof, demanded of those that stood by him why they were so amazed. I showed him how the cross had fallen upon Doctor Bonner's head. Quoth my Lord:

'Hath it drawn any blood?'

'Yea,' quoth I.

With that he cast down his head and soberly said 'Malum omen,' aad thereupon suddenly said grace, rose from table and went to his bedchamber, but what he did there I cannot tell. Now mark how my Lord expounded the meaning thereof to me at Pontefract after his fall. First that the great cross that he bore as Archbishop of York betokened himself, and Doctor Augustine the Physician, who overthrew the cross, was he that accused my Lord, whereby his enemies caught an occasion to overthrow him. It fell on Doctor Bonner's head, who was then master of my Lord's faculties and spiritual jurisdiction, and, moreover, the drawing of blood betokeneth death, which did suddenly after follow.

Now the appointed time drew near for Installation. Sitting at dinner the Friday before the Monday that he should have been installed at York, the Earl of Northumberland and Mr. Walshe with a great company of gentlemen of the Earl's house and of the country whom they had gathered in the King's name to accompany them, came to the hall of Cawood (the officers being then at dinner), and my Lord, not having fully dined, knew nothing of the Earl's coming.

The first thing that the Earl did after he had set

the hall in order was to command the porter to deliver the keys of the gate to him, which he would in no wise do, although he was threatened and commanded in the King's name to make deliverance thereof to one of the Earl's servants, which he still refused to do, saying to the Earl that the keys were delivered to him by his Lord and Master both by oath and under command.

Now, some of the gentlemen that stood by the Earl, hearing the porter speak so stoutly, said: 'He is a good fellow and a faithful servant to his master, and speaks like an honest man, therefore give him your charge and let him keep the keys still.' Then said the Earl: 'Thou shalt well and truly keep the keys to the use of our Sovereign Lord the King, and you shall let none pass in or out of the gates but such as from time to time you shall be commanded by us, being the King's Commissioners, during our stay here;' and with that oath he received the keys of the Earl at Master Walshe's hands. But of all these doings knew my Lord nothing, for they had stopped the stairs that none should go to my Lord's chamber, and they that came down could not go up again. At length one escaped up and showed my Lord that the Earl of Northumberland was in the hall, whereat my Lord wondered, and at first believed not till he heard it confirmed by another. Then quoth my

Lord: 'I am sorry we have dined, for I fear our officers have not provided fish enough for his entertainment with some honourable cheer fitting his estate and dignity.' But with that my Lord rose from the table and commanded to let the cloth lie that the Earl might see how far forward they were at their dinners, and as he was going down the stairs he encountered with my Lord of Northumberland, to whom my Lord said:

'You are heartily welcome, my Lord;' and so they embraced each other.

Then quoth my Lord Cardinal:

'If you had loved me, you would have sent me word before of your coming, that I might have entertained you according to your honour. Notwithstanding, you shall have such cheer as I can make you for the present with a right good will, trusting you will accept thereof in good part, and hoping hereafter to see you oftener, when I shall be more able to entertain you.'

This said, my Lord took him by the hand and led him to his chamber, followed by all the Earls and servants; and they were there all alone, saving I, which kept the door as my office required, being Gentleman Usher. While these two Lords stood at the window, the Earl, trembling, said:

'I arrest you of high treason.'

With which words my Lord was well-nigh

astonished, standing still a good space without speaking a word. But at the last quoth my Lord:

'What authority have you to arrest me?'

Quoth the Earl:

'I have a commission so to do.'

'Show it me,' quoth my Lord, 'that I may see the contents thereof.'

'Nay, sir, that you may not,' quoth the Earl.

Then quoth my Lord:

'Hold you contented, for I will not obey your arrest, for there hath been between your ancestors and my predecessors great contentions and debate. Therefore, unless I see your authority, I will not obey you.'

Even as they were debating the matter in the chamber, so likewise was Mr. Walshe busy in arresting Doctor Augustine at the door, saying:

'Go in, thou traitor, or I shall make thee!'

With that I opened the portal door, and he did thrust Doctor Augustine in before him with violence. The matter on both sides astonished me very much, marvelling what all this should mean, until at last Master Walshe, having entered my Lord's chamber, began to pluck off his hood, being of the same cloth as his coat, which hood he wore to the intent he should not be known, who kneeled down to my Lord, to whom my Lord said:

'Come hither, sir, and let me speak with you;' and commanding him to stand up, said thus: 'My Lord of Northumberland hath arrested me, but by what authority I know not. If you be privy thereunto and joined with him therein, I pray you show me.'

'Indeed, my Lord, if it please your Grace, I pray have me excused. There is annexed to our commission certain instructions such as you may not see nor be privy to.'

'Why,' quoth my Lord, 'be your instructions such as I may not see nor be privy thereunto, yet peradventure if I be privy unto them I may help you the better to perform them, for it is not unknown to you that I have been of counsel in as weighty matters as these are, and I doubt not I shall prove myself to be a true man against the expectation of my cruel enemies. I have an understanding whereupon all this matter groweth. Well, there is no more to do, I trow. You are of the Privy Chamber; your name is Master Walshe. I am contented to yield to you, but not to the Earl without I see his commission, and you are also a sufficient Commissioner in this behalf, being one of the Privy Chamber. Therefore, put your commission in execution; spare me not. I will obey you and the King, for I fear not the cruelty of mine enemies no more than I do the truth of my allegiance, wherein I take God to witness I never offended His Majesty in word or deed, and therein I dare stand face to face with any having a difference without partiality.'

Then came my Lord of Northumberland and commanded me to avoid the chamber, and being loath to depart from my master, I stood still and would not remove. Then he spake again, and said:

'There is no remedy; you must depart.'

With that I looked upon my master as one who would have said, 'Shall I go?' and perceiving by his countenance that it was not for me to stay, I departed and went into another chamber, where there were many gentlemen and others to hear news, to whom I made a report of what I heard and saw, which was great heaviness to them all.

Then the Earl called into his chamber divers of his own servants, and after he and Master Walshe had taken the keys from my Lord, he committed the keeping of my Lord unto five gentlemen, and then they went about the house and put all things in order, intending to depart next day and to certify to the King and the rest of the Lords what they had done.

Then went they busily about to convey Doctor Augustine away to London, with as much speed and privacy as possible, sending with him divers persons to conduct him, who was bound to his horse like a traitor.

And this being done, when it was near night, the Commissioners sending two grooms of my Lord's to attend him to his chamber (where he lay all night), the rest of the Earl's men watched in the chamber, and all the house was watched and the gates safe kept, that no man could pass or repass until the next morning.

About eight of the clock next morning the Earl sent for me into his chamber, and commanded me to go to my Lord, and as I was going, I met with Master Walshe, who called me unto him and showed me how the King's Majesty bore unto me his principal favour for my love and diligent service that I had performed to my Lord. 'Wherefore,' quoth he, 'the King's pleasure is that you shall be about him as chief, in whom His Highness putteth great confidence and trust.' And thereupon he gave me in writing the Articles, which, when I had read, I said I was content to obey His Majesty's pleasure, and would be sworn to the performance thereof, whereupon he gave me my oath.

That done, I resorted to my Lord, whom I found sitting in a chair, the table being ready spread for him. But so soon as he perceived me come in, he fell into such a woeful lamentation, that would have forced a flinty heart to mourn. I then comforted him as well as I could, but he would not.

'For,' quoth he, 'I am much grieved that I have nothing with which to reward you and the rest of my true and faithful servants, for all the good service they and you have done me, for which I do much lament.'

Upon Sunday following, the Earl and Master Walshe appointed to set forward, for my Lord's horse and ours were brought ready into the inner court, where we mounted and came towards the gate ready to ride out. The porter had no sooner opened the same, but we saw without ready attending a great number of gentlemen and their servants, such as the Earl had appointed for that service, to attend and conduct my Lord to Pomfret that night.

But to tell you the truth, there were also many of the rich people of the country assembled at the gate, lamenting his departure, in number about 3,000, who after they had a sight of him, cried out with a loud voice, 'God save your Grace! God save your Grace! The foul evil take them that have taken you from us! We pray God that vengeance may come upon them!' And thus they ran after him through the town of Cawood, for he was very well-beloved there, both of rich and poor.

XX

OF THE CARDINAL'S ENTERTAINMENT AT THE EARL OF SHREWSBURY'S, AND OF HIS DEATH AND BURIAL AT LEICESTER

AFTER our departure from Cawood we came to Doncaster; the third day we came to Sheffield Park, where my Lord of Shrewsbury lived within the Lodge, and the Earl and his lady and a great company of gentlewomen and servants stood without the gate to attend my Lord's coming, at whose alighting the Earl received him with much honour, and embracing him, said these words:

'My Lord, you are most heartily welcome to my poor Lodge, and I am glad to see you.'

Here my Lord stayed a fortnight, and was most nobly entertained; he spent most of his time and applied his mind to prayers continually, in great devotion. It came to pass as he sat one day at dinner, I, being there, perceived his colour divers times to change. I asked if he was not well. He answered me with a loud voice:

'I am suddenly taken with a thing at my stomach, and am not well. Therefore take up the table and make a short dinner, and return to me again at once.'

I made but little stay, but came to him again, and found him still sitting very ill at ease. He desired me to go to the apothecary and ask him if he had anything that would break wind upwards. He told me he had; then I went and showed the same to my Lord, who did command me to give him some thereof, and so I did, and it made him break wind exceedingly.

'Lo,' quoth he, 'you may see it was but the wind, for now I thank God I am well eased.'

And so he arose from the table and went to prayers, as he used every day after dinner.

In the afternoon my Lord of Shrewsbury sent for me to him and said:

'Forasmuch as I have always perceived you to be a man in whom my Lord putteth great confidence, and I myself knowing you to be a very honest man' (with many words of commendations and praise more than becometh me to rehearse), 'I would tell you that your Lord and Master hath often desired me to write unto the King, that he might answer his accusations before his enemies.

And this day I have received letters from His Majesty by Sir William Kingston, whereby I perceive that the King hath him in good opinion, and upon my request hath sent for him by the said Sir William Kingston. Therefore now I would have you play your part wisely with him, in such sort as he may take it quietly and in good part, for he is always full of sorrow and heaviness at my being with him, that I fear he would take it ill if I bring him tidings thereof. And therein doth he not well, for I assure you that the King is his very good Lord, and hath given me most hearty thanks for his entertainment. Therefore go your way to him in quiet till my coming, for I will not tarry long after you.'

'Sir,' quoth I, 'if it please your Lordship, I shall endeavour to the best of my power to accomplish your Lordship's command. But, sir, I doubt when I name this Sir William Kingston that he will guess some ill, because he is Constable of the Tower and Captain of the Guard, having in his company twenty-four of the Guard to accompany him.'

'That is nothing,' quoth the Earl. 'What if he be Constable of the Tower and Captain of the Guard, he is the fittest man for his wisdom and discretion to be sent about such a business; and as for the Guard, it is only to defend him from those that might intend him any ill. Besides that, the Guard are for the most part such of his old servants as the King hath taken into his service to attend him most justly.'

'Well, sir,' quoth I, 'I shall do what I can;' and so I departed and went to my Lord, and found him in the gallery with his staff and his beads in his hands. Seeing me come, he asked me what news I had. 'Forsooth,' quoth I, 'the best news that ever you heard, if you can take it well.'

'I pray God it be true then,' quoth he.

'My Lord of Shrewsbury,' said I, 'your most assured friend, hath so provided by his letters to the King that His Majesty hath sent for you by Master Kingston and twenty-four of the Guard to conduct you to His Highness.'

'Master Kingston!' quoth he, while he clapped his hand on his thigh and gave a great sigh.

'May it please your Grace,' quoth I, 'I would you would take all things well—it would be much better for you; content yourself, for God's sake, and think that God and your good friends have wrought for you according to your desires. And you have much more cause to rejoice than lament or mistrust the matter, for I assure you that your friends are more afraid of you than you need be of them. And His Majesty, to show his love to you, hath sent Master Kingston to honour you with as much honour as is your Grace's due, and to convey you in such easy journeys as is fitting for you and as you shall command. And I humbly entreat you to take to heart this my persuasion in His Highness's discretion, and to be of good cheer, wherewith you shall comfort yourself and give your friends and poor servants great comfort and content.'

'Well,' quoth he, 'I perceive more than you can imagine or do know.'

Presently after came my Lord to acquaint him with that I had so lately related. My Lord Cardinal thanked the Earl for his great love and called for Master Kingston, who came to him presently, and, kneeling down before him, saluted him in the King's behalf, whom my Lord bareheaded offered to take up, but he would not. Then quoth my Lord :

'Master Kingston, I pray you stand up and leave your kneeling to me, for I am a wretch, full of misery, not esteeming myself but as a mere object utterly cast away, without desert ; therefore, good Master Kingston, stand up.'

Then Master Kingston said :

'The King's Majesty hath him commended unto you.'

'I thank His Highness,' quoth my Lord ; 'I hope he is in good health.'

'Yea,' quoth Master Kingston, 'he has commanded me to bid you be of good cheer, for he beareth you as much goodwill as ever he did; and whereas report hath been made unto him that you should commit against His Majesty certain heinous crimes which he thinketh to be untrue, yet he, for the ministration of justice in such cases requisite, could do no less than send for you that you might have your trial, mistrusting nothing your truth and wisdom, but that you shall be able to acquit yourself of all complaints and accusations extended against you. You may take your journey to him at your pleasure, commanding me to attend you.'

'Master Kingston,' quoth my Lord, 'I thank you for your good news, and, sir, hereof assure yourself, if I were as able and lusty as ever I was to ride, I would go with you post, but alas! I am a diseased man, having a flux, that maketh me very weak; but the comfortable news you bring is of purpose to bring me into a fool's paradise, for I know what is provided for me. Notwithstanding, I thank you for your goodwill and pains taken about me, and I shall with speed make ready to ride with you.'

After this I was commanded to make all things ready for our departure the morrow after.

When my Lord went to bed he fell very sick,

and the opinions of the physicians were that he had not above four or five days to live. Notwithstanding, he would have ridden with Master Kingston next day, had not the Earl of Shrewsbury advised him to the contrary; but the following day after he took his journey with Master Kingston and them of the Guard, who, seeing him, could not abstain from weeping, considering he was their old master and now in such miserable case. My Lord took them by the hand, and would as he rode by the way sometimes talk with one and sometimes with another, till he came to a house of my Lord's standing in the way called Hardwick Hall, where he lay all that night very ill at ease.

The next day he came to Nottingham, and the next day to Leicester Abbey. The following day he waxed very sick, so that he had almost fallen from his horse, and it was night ere he got to Leicester Abbey, where, at his coming in at the gates, the Abbot with all the convent met him with many lighted torches, whom they honourably received and welcomed with great reverence.

My Lord said, 'Father Abbot, I am come to lay my bones amongst you,' he meanwhile riding still on his mule till he came to the stairs of his chamber, where he alighted.

Master Kingston, holding him by the arm, led

him upstairs, who told me after that he never felt so heavy a burden in all his life. And as soon as my Lord was in his chamber he went straight to bed. This was upon Saturday, and so he continued. On Monday in the morning, as I stood by his bedside about eight of the clock, the windows being close shut, and having wax-lights burning upon the cupboard, I thought I perceived him drawing on towards death. He, perceiving my shadow at the bedside, asked who was there.

'Sir,' quoth I, 'it is I.'

'How do you?' quoth he.

'Well, sir, if I might see your Grace well.'

'What is it a clock?' quoth he.

I answered it was about eight of the clock.

Quoth he, 'That cannot be,' saying the same words divers time. 'It cannot be eight of the clock, for by eight of the clock you shall see your master's time draw near that I must depart this world.'

With that, Doctor Palmes, a worthy gentleman standing by, bid me ask him if he would be shriven to make him ready for God, whatever chanced to fall out. This I did, but he was very angry with me, and asked what I had to do to ask him such a question, till at last Master Doctor took my part and talked with him in Latin and pacified him.

After dinner Master Kingston sent for me and said:

'Sir, the King hath sent unto me letters by Master Vincent, our old companion, who hath been in trouble in the Tower for money that my Lord should have at his departure, a great part of which money cannot be found, wherefore the King, at Master Vincent's request for the declaration of the truth, hath sent him hither with His Grace's letter that I should examine my Lord and have your counsel therein, that he may take it well and in good part. And this is the cause of my sending for you; therefore I desire your counsel therein for acquittal of this poor gentleman, Master Vincent.'

'Sir,' quoth I, 'according to my duty and by my advice, you shall resort unto him in your own person to visit him, and in communication break the matter unto him, and if he will not tell you the truth therein, then you may certify the King thereof, but in any case name not nor speak of my fellow Vincent. Also I would not have you delay, for he is very sick, and I fear he will not live past a day or two'; and accordingly Master Kingston went to my Lord and demanded the money, saying that 'my Lord of Northumberland found in a book at Cawood House that you had lately borrowed £1,000, and there is not so much as one penny to be found. Wherefore the King hath written to me to know what is become thereof, for it were pity that it should be holden from you both. Therefore I require you in the King's name to tell me the truth, that I may make a just report thereof unto His Majesty of your answer.'

With that quoth my Lord:

'O good Lord, how much doth it grieve me that the King should think any such thing of me, that I should deceive him of one penny, seeing I have nothing nor ever had (God be my judge) that I ever esteemed so much my own as His Majesty's, having but the bare use of it during my life, and after my death to leave it wholly to him, wherein His Majesty hath prevented me. But for this money that you demand of me, I assure you it is none of my own, for I borrowed it of divers of my friends to bury me, and to bestow amongst my servants who have taken great pains about me; notwithstanding, if it be your pleasure to know, I must be content, yet I beseech His Majesty to see them satisfied of whom I borrowed the same, for the discharge of my conscience.'

'Who be they?' quoth Master Kingston.

'That shall I tell you,' quoth my Lord. 'I borrowed two hundred pounds of John Allen of London, another two hundred pounds of Sir Richard Gresham, and two hundred pounds of Doctor Hickden, Dean of my College at Oxford;

two hundred pounds of Mr. Ellis, my Chaplain, and another two hundred pounds of a priest. I hope the King will restore it again, forasmuch as it is none of mine.'

'Sir,' quoth Master Kingston, 'there is no doubt in the King, whom you need not distrust; but, sir, I pray you where is the money?'

Quoth he:

'I will not conceal it, I warrant you, but I will declare it unto you before I die, by the grace of God. Have a little patience with me, I pray you, for the money is safe enough in an honest man's hands, who will not keep one penny thereof from the King.'

So Master Kingston departed for that time, my Lord being very weak, and about four of the clock next morning I asked him how he did.

'Well,' quoth he, 'if I had any meat. I pray you give me some.'

'Sir,' quoth I, 'there is none ready.'

Then he said:

'You are much to blame; you should always have meat for me in readiness, whensoever that my stomach serves me. I pray you get some ready for me, for I mean to make myself strong to-day, to the intent I may go to confession and make me ready for God.'

Quoth I, 'I will call up the cooks to prepare

some meat, and also I will call Mr. Palmes, that he may discourse with you till your meat be ready.'

'With a good will,' quoth he.

And so I called Master Palmes, who rose and came to my Lord. Then I went and acquainted Master Kingston that my Lord was very sick, and not like to live.

'In good faith!' quoth Master Kingston, 'you are much to blame to make him believe he is sicker than he is.'

'Well, sir,' quoth I, 'you cannot but say I gave you warning, as I am bound to do.'

Upon which words he arose and came unto him; but before he came my Lord Cardinal had eaten a spoonful or two of cullis made of chicken, and after that he was at his confession the space of an hour. And then Master Kingston came to him and bid him good morrow, and asked him how he did.

'Sir,' quoth he, 'I watch but God's pleasure to render up my poor soul to Him. I pray you have me heartily commended unto his royal Majesty, and beseech him on my behalf to call to his princely remembrance all matters that have been between us from the beginning, and the progress, and especially between good Queen Katherine and him, and then shall His Grace's conscience know whether I have offended him or not. He is a Prince of a most royal carriage, and hath a princely heart, and rather than he will miss or want any part of his will he will endanger the one-half of his kingdom.

'I do assure you I have often knelt before him, sometimes three hours together, to persuade him from his will and appetite, and could not prevail. And, Master Kingston, had I but served God as diligently as I have served the King, He would not have given me over in my gray hairs. But this is the just reward that I must receive for my diligent pains and study, not regarding my service to God, but only to my Prince. Therefore, let me advise you, if you be one of the Privy Council, as by your wisdom you are fit, take heed what you put in the King's head, for you can never put it out again.

'And I desire you further to request His Grace in God's name that he have a vigilant eye to suppress the hellish Lutherans, that they increase not through his great negligence, in such a sort as he be compelled to take up arms to subdue them, as the King of Bohemia was, whose commons being infected with Wickliff's heresies, the King was forced to take that course.

'Let him consider the story of King Richard II., the second son of his progenitor, who lived in the time of Wickliff's seditions and heresies. Did not the commons, I pray you, in his time rise against the nobility and chief governors of this realm, and at the last some of them were put to death without justice or mercy; and under pretence of having all things in common, did they not fall to spoiling and robbing, and at last took the King's person and carried him about the city, making him obedient to their proclamations?

'Did not also the traitorous heretic Sir John Oldcastle, Lord Cobham, pitch a field with heretics against Henry IV., where the King was in person, and fought against them, to whom God gave the victory.

'Alas! if these be not plain precedents and sufficient persuasions to admonish a prince, then God will take away from us our prudent rulers, and leave us to the hands of our enemies. And then will ensue mischief, inconveniences, barrenness, and scarcity, for want of good orders in the Commonwealth, from which God of His tender mercy defend us!

'Master Kingston, farewell! I wish all things may have good success. My time draws on; I may not tarry with you. I pray you remember my words.'

Now began the time to draw near, and his tongue began to fail him; his eyes were perfectly set in his head, and his sight failed him. Then we began to put him in mind of Christ's Passion, and caused the Yeomen of the Guard to stand by privately, to see him die, and bear witness of his words and his departure, who heard all his communications. And then presently the clock struck eight, at which time he gave up the ghost, and thus departed he this life, each of us looking on one another, supposing he prophesied of his departure. We sent for the Abbot of the house to anoint him, who speedily came as he was ending his life, who said certain prayers before that the life was out of his body.

The Cardinal being departed, Master Kingston sent post to London one of the Guard. Then was Master Kingston and the Abbot in consultation about the funeral, which was solemnized the day after, for Master Kingston would not stay the return of the post.

They thought good that the Mayor of Leicester and his brethren should personally see him dead, to prevent false reports that he was alive. And in the interim, whilst the Mayor was sent for, his bones were laid in a coffin, and his shirt of hair and his over-shirt of fine holland were taken off and were put into the coffin together with all such ornaments wherewith he was invested when he was made Archbishop, as mitre, cross, ring and pall, and all other things appertaining to his office.

Thus he lay all that day with his coffin open and barefaced, that all that desired might see him. And about three of the clock he was buried by the Abbot with great solemnity; and his corpse was set in the Lady-chapel of the church with many tapers and poor men about him holding the torches in their hands, who watched the corpse all that night whilst the Canons sung divers dirges and other Divine orisons.

And at four of the clock next morning the Cardinal's servants and Master Kingston came to the church to the execution of many ceremonies in such manner as is usual at Bishops' burials, and that done Master Kingston went to Mass, where the Abbot did offer and divers others; and then they went to bury the corpse in the middle of the said Chapel. By this time it was six of the clock, being St. Andrew's Day.

Then we prepared for our journey to the Court, where we attended His Majesty. The next day I was sent for to the King, conducted by Master Norris, and the King was in his nightgown of velvet furred with sables, before whom I knelt the space of an hour, during which time His Majesty examined me of divers particulars concerning my Lord Cardinal, wishing rather than twenty thousand pounds that he had lived.

He asked me concerning the fifteen hundred

pounds which Master Kingston had spoken of to my Lord. Quoth I:

'I think I can perfectly tell your Grace where it is, and who hath it.'

'Can you?' quoth the King. 'I pray tell me, and you shall not be unrewarded.'

'Sir,' quoth I, 'after the departure of Master Vincent from my Lord at Scroby, who had the custody thereof, leaving it with my Lord in divers bags, he delivered it to a certain priest safely to be kept for his use.'

'Is this true?' quoth the King.

'Yea,' quoth I; 'without doubt the priest will not deny it before me, for I was at the delivery thereof, who hath got divers other rich ornaments which are not registered in the book of my Lord's inventory or other writings whereby any man is able to charge him therewith but myself.'

Then said the King:

'Let me alone, and keep this secret between you and me, and let no man be privy thereof; for your honesty and truth you shall be our servant in our chamber as you were with your master. Therefore go your ways to Sir John Gage, our Vice-Chamberlain, to whom we have spoken already to admit you our servant, in our chamber, and then go to the Lord of Norfolk, and he shall pay you your whole year's was, which is ten pounds. Is it not so?' quoth the King.

'Yes, forsooth, and if it please your grace,' quoth I.

And said the King:

'You shall receive a reward of the Duke of Norfolk.'

So I received ten pounds of the Duke for my wages and twenty pounds for my reward, and His Majesty gave me a cart and six horses, the best that I could choose out of my Lord's horses, to carry my goods, and five marks for my charge homewards.

THE END

R. & T. Washbourne, 18 Paternoster Row, London

LL
xo viel
seku